CW00501225

# 1 MONTH OF FREE READING

at

**www.ForgottenBooks.com**

By purchasing this book you are eligible for one month membership to ForgottenBooks.com, giving you unlimited access to our entire collection of over 1,000,000 titles via our web site and mobile apps.

To claim your free month visit:

www.forgottenbooks.com/free840424

* Offer is valid for 45 days from date of purchase. Terms and conditions apply.

ISBN 978-0-365-37261-5
PIBN 10840424

This book is a reproduction of an important historical work. Forgotten Books uses state-of-the-art technology to digitally reconstruct the work, preserving the original format whilst repairing imperfections present in the aged copy. In rare cases, an imperfection in the original, such as a blemish or missing page, may be replicated in our edition. We do, however, repair the vast majority of imperfections successfully; any imperfections that remain are intentionally left to preserve the state of such historical works.

Forgotten Books is a registered trademark of FB &c Ltd.
Copyright © 2018 FB &c Ltd.
FB &c Ltd, Dalton House, 60 Windsor Avenue, London, SW19 2RR.
Company number 08720141. Registered in England and Wales.

For support please visit www.forgottenbooks.com

# A
# TOUR
## THROUGH
# SICILY AND MALTA.

VOL. II.

NEW YORK
PUBLIC
LIBRARY

# A
# TOUR
THROUGH
# SICILY AND MALTA.

IN A
SERIES OF LETTERS
TO
WILLIAM BECKFORD, Esq.
OF SOMERLY IN SUFFOLK;
FROM
P. BRYDONE, F.R.S.

THE SECOND EDITION, CORRECTED.

VOL. II.

NEW YORK PUBLIC LIBRARY

LONDON:
PRINTED FOR W. STRAHAN; AND
T. CADELL, IN THE STRAND.
MDCCLXXIV.

THE NEW YORK
PUBLIC LIBRARY
70[illegible]
ASTOR, LENOX AND
TILDEN FOUNDATIONS.
1897.

# CONTENTS

OF THE

## SECOND VOLUME.

LET-

LET-

LET-

LET-

6 *Method*

# A
# TOUR
## THROUGH
# SICILY AND MALTA.

## LETTER XVII.

DEAR BECKFORD, Agrigentum, June 11th.

WE left the port of Malta in a ſparonaro which we hired to convey us to this city.

We coaſted along the iſland, and went to take a view of the north-port, its fortifications and lazaretto. All theſe are very great, and more like the works of a mighty and powerful people, than of ſo ſmall a ſtate. The mortars cut out of the rock are a tremendous invention. There are about fifty of them, near the different creeks and landing-places round the iſland. They are directed at the moſt probable ſpots where boats would attempt a landing. The mouths of ſome of theſe mortars are about ſix feet wide, and they are ſaid to throw a hundred cantars of cannon-ball or ſtones. A cantar is, I think, about a hundred pound weight; ſo that if they do take place, they muſt make a dreadful havoc amongſt a debarkation of boats.

The diſtance of Malta from Gozzo is not above four or five miles, and the ſmall iſland of Commino lies betwixt them. The coaſts of all the three are bare and barren, but covered over with towers, redoubts, and fortifications of various kinds.

As Gozzo is ſuppoſed to be the celebrated iſland of Calypſo, you may believe we expected

pected something very fine; but we were disappointed. It must either be greatly fallen off since the time she inhabited it; or the archbishop of Cambray, as well as Homer, must have flattered greatly in their painting. We looked, as we went along the coast, for the grotto of the goddess; but could see nothing that resembled it. Neither could we observe those verdant banks eternally covered with flowers; nor those lofty trees for ever in blossom, that lost their heads in the clouds, and afforded a shade to the sacred baths of her and her nymphs. We saw, indeed, some nymphs; but as neither Calypso nor Eucharis seemed to be of the number, we paid little attention to them, and I was in no apprehension about my Telemachus: Indeed, it would have required an imagination as strong as Don Quixote's, to have brought about the metamorphosis.

Finding our hopes frustrated, we ordered our sailors to pull out to sea, and bid adieu to the iſland of Calypſo, concluding, either that our intelligence was falſe, or that both the iſland and its inhabitants were greatly changed. We ſoon found ourſelves once more at the mercy of the waves: Night came on, and our rowers began their evening ſong to the Virgin, and beat time with their oars. Their offering was acceptable; for we had the moſt delightful weather. We wrapt ourſelves up in our cloaks, and ſlept moſt comfortably, having provided mattraſſes at Malta. By a little after day-break, we found we had got without ſight of all the iſlands, and ſaw only a part of mount Ætna ſmoking above the waters. The wind ſprung up fair, and by ten o'clock we had ſight of the coaſt of Sicily.

On conſidering the ſmallneſs of our boat, and the great breadth of this paſſage, we could not help admiring the temerity of theſe people, who, at all ſeaſons of the year, venture to Sicily in theſe diminutive

veſſels;

vessels; yet it is very seldom that any accident happens; they are so perfectly acquainted with the weather, foretelling, almost to a certainty, every storm, many hours before it comes on. The sailors look upon this passage as one of the most stormy and dangerous in the Mediterranean. It is called the canal of Malta, and is much dreaded by the Levant ships; but indeed, at this season, there is no danger.

We arrived at Sicily a little before sunset, and landed opposite to Ragusa, and not far from the ruins of the little Hybla; the third town of that name in the island, distinguished by the epithets of the Great, (near mount Ætna) the Lesser, (near Augusta) and the Little (just by Ragusa). Here we found a fine sandy beach, and and whilst the servants were employed in dressing supper, we amused ourselves with bathing and gathering shells, of which there is a considerable variety. We were in expectation of finding the nautilus, for which this island is famous; but in this we did not succeed. However, we picked up some handsome shells, though not equal to those that are brought from the Indies.

After supper, we again launched our bark, and went to sea. The wind was favourable as we could wish. We had our nightly serenade as usual, and the next day, by twelve o'clock, we reached the celebrated port of Agrigentum.

The captain of the port gave us a polite reception, and insisted on accompanying us to the city, which stands near the top of a mountain, four miles distant from the harbour, and about eleven hundred feet above the level of the sea. The road on each side is bordered by a row of exceeding large American aloes; upwards of one-third of them being at present in full blow, and making the most beautiful appearance

pearance that can be imagined. The flower-stems of this noble plant are in general betwixt twenty and thirty feet high, (some of them more) and are covered with flowers from top to bottom; which taper regularly, and form a beautiful kind of pyramid, the base or pedestal of which is the fine spreading leaves of the plant. As this is esteemed in northern countries, one of the greatest curiosities of the vegetable tribe, we were happy at seeing it in so great perfection; much greater, I think, than I had ever seen it before.

With us, I think, it is vulgarly reckoned, (though I believe falsely) that they only flower once in a hundred years. Here I was informed, that, at the latest, they always blow the sixth year; but for the most part the fifth.—As the whole substance of the plant is carried into the stem and the flowers, the leaves begin to decay as soon as the blow is completed, and a numerous offspring of young plants are produced round the root of the old one; these are ſlip'd off, and formed into new plantations, either for hedges or for avenues to their country-houſes.

The city of Agrigentum, now called *Girgenti*, is irregular and ugly; though from a few miles diſtance at ſea, it makes a noble appearance, little inferior to that of Genoa.—As it lies on the ſlope of the mountain, the houſes do not hide one another; but every part of the city is ſeen.

On our arrival, we found a great falling off indeed; the houſes are mean, the ſtreets dirty, crooked, and narrow.—It ſtill contains near twenty thouſand people; a ſad reduction from its antient grandeur, when it was ſaid to conſiſt of no leſs than eight hundred thouſand, being the next city to Syracuſe for numbers.

The

The Canonico Spoto, from Mr. Hamilton's letter, and from our former acquaintance with him at Naples, gave us a kind, and a hoſpitable reception. He inſiſted on our being his gueſts; and we are now in his houſe, comfortably lodged, and elegantly entertained, which, after our crowded little apartment in the ſparonaro, is by no means a diſagreeable change.—Farewell.—I ſhall write you again ſoon.

Ever yours.

## LETTER XVIII.

Agrigentum, June 12th.

WE are just now returned from examining the antiquities of Agrigentum, the most considerable, perhaps, of any in Sicily.

The ruins of the antient city lie about a short mile from the modern one. These, like the ruins of Syracuse, are mostly converted into corn-fields, vineyards, and orchards; but the remains of the temples here, are much more conspicuous than those of Syracuse. Four of these have stood pretty much in a right line, near the south wall of the city. The first they call the temple of Venus; almost one half of which still remains. The second is that of Concord: It may be considered as entire, not one column having as yet fallen. It is

precisely

precisely of the same dimensions and same architecture as that of Venus, which had probably served as the model for it. By the following inscription, found on a large piece of marble, it appears to have been built at the expence of the Lilibitani; probably after having been defeated by the people of Agrigentum.

CONCORDIÆ AGRIGENTINORUM SACRUM,
RESPUBLICA LILIBITANORUM,
DEDICANTIBUS M. ATTERIO CANDIDQ
PROCOS. ET L. CORNELIO MAR.
CELLO. Q. P. R. P. R.

These temples are supported by thirteen large fluted Doric columns on each side; and six at each end. All their bases, capitals, entablatures, &c. still remain entire; and as the architecture is perfectly simple, without any thing affected or studied, the whole strikes the eye at once, and pleases very much. The columns are, indeed, shorter than the common Doric proportions; and

and they certainly are not ſo elegant as ſome of the antient temples near Rome, and in other places in Italy.

The third temple is that of Hercules, altogether in ruins; but appears to have been of a much greater ſize than the former two. We meaſured ſome of the broken columns, near ſeven feet in diameter. It was here that the famous ſtatue of Hercules ſtood, ſo much celebrated by Cicero; which the people of Agrigentum defended with ſuch bravery, againſt Verres, who attempted to ſeize it. You will find the whole ſtory in his pleadings againſt that infamous prætor.

There was likewiſe in this temple a famous picture by Zeuxis. Hercules was repreſented in his cradle killing the two ſerpents: Alcmena and Amphitrion having juſt entered the apartment, were painted with every mark of terror and aſtoniſhment.

ment. Pliny ſays, the painter looked upon this piece as invaluable; and therefore could never be prevailed on to put a price upon it, but gave it as a preſent to Agrigentum, to be placed in the temple of Hercules. Theſe two great maſter-pieces have been loſt. We thought of them with regret, whilſt we trod on theſe venerable ruins.

Near to this lie ruins of the temple of Jupiter Olympus, ſuppoſed, by the Sicilian authors, to have been the largeſt in the heathen world. It is now called *il tempio de' giganti*, or the Giants Temple, as the people cannot conceive that ſuch maſſes of rock could ever be put together by the hands of ordinary men. The fragments of columns are indeed enormous, and give us a vaſt idea of this fabric. It is ſaid to have ſtood till the year 1100; but is now a perfect ruin. Our Cicerones aſſured us, it was exactly the ſame dimenſions with the church of St. Peter at Rome: But in this they are egregiously mistaken.—St. Peter's being much greater than any thing that ever the heathen world produced.

There are the remains of many more temples, and other great works; but these, I think, are the most conspicuous. They shew you that of Vulcan, of Proserpine, of Castor and Pollux, and a very remarkable one of Juno. This too was enriched by one of the most famous pictures of antiquity; which is celebrated by many of the antient writers.—Zeuxis was determined to excel every thing that had gone before him, and to form a model of human perfection. To this end, he prevailed on all the finest women of Agrigentum, who were even ambitious of the honour, to appear naked before him. Of these he chose five for his models, and moulding all the perfections of these beauties into one, he composed the picture of the goddess. This was ever looked upon on as his master-piece; but was unfortunately burnt when the Carthaginians took Agrigentum.—Many of the citizens retired into this temple as to a place of safety; but as soon as they found the gates attacked by the enemy, they agreed to set fire to it; and chose rather to perish in the flames, than submit to the power of the conquerors. However, neither the destruction of the temple, nor the loss of their lives, has been so much regretted by posterity, as the loss of this picture.

The temple of Æsculapius (the ruins of which are still to be seen) was not less celebrated for a statue of Apollo. It was taken from them by the Carthaginians at the same time that the temple of Juno was burnt. It was carried off by the conquerors, and continued the greatest ornament of Carthage for many years, and was at last restored by Scipio, at the final destruction of that city. Some of the Sicilians allege, I believe without any ground, that it was afterwards carried to Rome, and ſtill remains there, the wonder of all ages; known to the whole world under the name of the Apollo of Belvidere; and allowed to be the perfection of human art.

I ſhould be very tedious, were I to give you a minute deſcription of every piece of antiquity. Indeed, little or nothing is to be learned from the greateſt part of them: The antient walls of the city are moſtly cut out of the rock; the catacombs and ſepulchres are all very great: One of theſe is worthy of particular notice, becauſe it is mentioned by Polybius, as being oppoſite to the temple of Hercules, and to have been ſtruck by lightning even in his time. It remains almoſt entire, and anſwers the deſcription he gives of it: The inſcriptions are ſo defaced, that we could make nothing of them.

This

This is the monument of Tero king of Agrigentum, one of the firſt of the Sicilian tyrants. The great antiquity of it may be gathered from this, that Tero is not only mentioned by Diodorus, Polybius, and the later of the antient hiſtorians; but likewiſe by Herodotus, and Pindar, who dedicates two of his Olympic odes to him: So that this monument muſt be more than two thouſand years old. It is a kind of pyramid, probably one of the moſt durable forms.

All theſe mighty ruins of Agrigentum, and the whole mountain on which it ſtands, are compoſed of a concretion of ſea-ſhells, run together, and cemented by a kind of ſand or gravel, and now become as hard, and perhaps more durable than even marble itſelf. This ſtone is white before it has been expoſed to the air; but in the temples and other ruins, it is become of a dark brown. I ſhall bring home ſome pieces of it for the inſpection of the curious. I found theſe ſhells on the very ſummit of the mountain, at leaſt fourteen or fifteen hundred feet above the level of the ſea. They are of the commoneſt kinds, cockles, muſſels, oyſters, &c.

> " The things we know are neither rich nor rare;
> " But wonder how the devil they got there."
>
> POPE.

By what means they have been lifted up to this vaſt height, and ſo intimately mixed with the ſubſtance of the rock, I leave to you and your philoſophical friends to determine.—This old battered globe of ours, has probably ſuffered many convulſions not recorded in any hiſtory.—You have heard of the vaſt Stratum of bones lately diſcovered in Iſtria and Oſſero;—part of it runs below rocks of marble, upwards of forty feet in thickneſs, and they have not yet been able to aſcertain its extent: Something of the ſame kind has been found in Dalmatia, in the iſlands of the Archipelago; and, lately, I am told, in the rock of Gibraltar.—Now, the deluge recorded in Scripture, will hardly account for all the appearances of this ſort to be met with, almoſt in every country in the world.—But I am interrupted by viſitors;—which is a lucky circumſtance, both for you and me; for I was juſt going to be very philoſophical, and conſequently very dull.—Adieu.

## LETTER XIX.

Agrigentum, June 13th.

THE interruption in my laſt, was a deputation from the biſhop, to invite us to a great dinner to-morrow at the port; ſo that we ſhall know whether this place ſtill deſerves the character of luxury, it always held amongſt the antients: We have great reaſon to think, from the politeneſs and attention we have met with, that it has never loſt its antient hoſpitality, for which it was likewiſe ſo much celebrated.

Plato, when he viſited Sicily, was ſo much ſtruck with the luxury of Agrigentum, both in their houſes and their tables, that a ſaying of his is ſtill recorded: That they built as if they were never to die, and eat as if they had not an hour to live.

It

It is preſerved by Ælian, and is juſt now before me.

He tells a ſtory by way of illuſtration, which ſhews a much greater conformity of manners than one could have expected, betwixt the young nobility amongſt the antients, and our own at this day.

He ſays, that after a great feaſt, where there was a number of young people of the firſt faſhion, they got all ſo much intoxicated, that from their reeling and tumbling upon one another, they imagined they were at ſea in a ſtorm, and began to think themſelves in the moſt imminent danger; at laſt they agreed, that the only way to ſave their lives was to lighten the ſhip, and with one accord began to throw the rich furniture out of the windows, to the great edification of the mob below; and did not ſtop till they had entirely cleared the houſe of it, which, from this exploit, was ever after denominated the *triremes*, or the ſhip. He ſays it was one of the principal palaces of the city, and retained this name for ever after. In Dublin, I have been told, there are more than one triremes; and that this frolic, which they call throwing the houſe out of the window, is by no means uncommon.

At the ſame time that Agrigentum is abuſed by the antient authors for its drunkenneſs, it is as much celebrated for its hoſpitality; and I believe, it will be found, that this virtue, and this vice, have ever had a ſort of ſneaking kindneſs for each other, and have generally gone hand in hand, both in antient and in modern times. The Swiſs, the Scotch, and the Iriſh, who are at preſent the moſt drunken people in Europe, are likewiſe, in all probability, the moſt hoſpitable; whereas, in the very ſober countries, Spain, Portugal, and Italy, hoſpitality is a virtue very little known, or indeed

indeed any other virtue, except sobriety; which has been produced, probably a good deal from the tyranny of their government, and their dread of the inquisition; for where every person is in fear, lest his real sentiments should appear, it would be very dangerous to unlock his heart; but in countries where there are neither civil nor ecclesiastical tyrants to lay an embargo on our thoughts, people are under no apprehension lest they should be known.

However, these are not the only reasons. The moral virtues and vices may sometimes depend on natural causes.—The very elevated situation of this city, where the air is exceedingly thin and cold, has perhaps been one reason why its inhabitants are fonder of wine than their neighbours in the valleys.

The same may be said of the three nations I have mentioned; the greatest part of their countries lying amongſt hills and mountains, where the climate renders ſtrong liquors more neceſſary; or, at leaſt, leſs pernicious, than in low places.—It is not ſurpriſing, that this practice, probably begun amongſt the mountains, where the air is ſo keen, has by degrees crept down into the valleys, and has at laſt become almoſt epidemical in thoſe countries.

Fazzello, after railing at Agrigentum for its drunkenneſs, adds, that there was no town in the iſland ſo celebrated for its hoſpitality. He ſays that many of the nobles had ſervants placed at the gates of the city, to invite all ſtrangers to their houſes. It is in reference to this probably, that Empedocles ſays, that even the gates of the city proclaimed a welcome to every ſtranger. From our experience we are well intitled to ſay, that the people of Agrigentum ſtill retain this antiquated virtue, ſo little known in polite countries. To-morrow we ſhall have

have a better opportunity of judging whether it is ſtill accompanied by its ſiſter vice.

The accounts that the old authors give of the magnificence of Agrigentum are amazing; though indeed there are none of them that proclaim it in ſtronger terms than the monuments that ſtill remain.—Diodorus ſays, the great veſſels for holding water were commonly of ſilver, and the litters and carriages for the moſt part were of ivory richly adorned. He mentions a pond made at an immenſe expence, full of fiſh and of water-fowl, that in his time was the great reſort of the inhabitants, on their feſtivals; but he ſays, that even then (in the age of Auguſtus) it was going to ruin, requiring too great an expence to keep it up. There is not now the ſmalleſt veſtige of it: But there is ſtill to be ſeen a curious ſpring of water that throws up a kind of oil on its ſurface, which

which is made uſe of by the poor people in many diſeaſes. This is ſuppoſed to mark out the place of the celebrated pond; which is recorded by Pliny and Solinus to have abounded with this oil.

Diodorus, ſpeaking of the riches of Agrigentum, mentions one of its citizens returning victorious from the Olympic games, and entering his city, attended by three hundred chariots, each drawn by four white horſes, richly capariſoned; and gives many other inſtances of their vaſt profuſion and luxury.

Thoſe horſes, according to that author, were eſteemed all over Greece, for their beauty and ſwiftneſs; and their race is celebrated by many of the antient writers.

" Arduus inde Agragas oſtentat maxima longe
" Moenia, magnanimum quondam generator
" equorum,"

ſays

says Virgil in the third Æneid; and Pliny acquaints us, that those which had been often victorious at the games were not only honoured with burial rites, but had magnificent monuments erected to eternize their memory. This Timeus confirms: He tells us, that he saw at Agrigentum several pyramids built as sepulchral monuments to celebrated horses; he adds that when those animals became old and unfit for service, they were always taken care of, and spent the remainder of their lives in ease and plenty.—I could wish that our countrymen would imitate the gratitude and humanity of the Sicilians in this article; at least, the latter part of it. I don't know that our nation can so justly be taxed with cruelty or ingratitude in any other article as in their treatment of horses, the animal that of all others is the most intitled to our care. How piteous a thing it is, on many of your great roads, to see the finest old hunters, that were once the glory

glory of the chace, condemned, in the decline of life, to the tyranny of the moſt cruel oppreſſors; in whoſe hands they ſuffer the moſt extreme miſery, till they at laſt ſink under the taſk that is aſſigned them. I am called away to ſee ſome more antiques, but ſhall finiſh this letter to-night, as the poſt goes off for Italy to-morrow morning.

13th; Afternoon. We have ſeen a great many old walls and vaults that little or nothing can be made of. They give them names, and pretend to tell you what they were, but as they bear no reſemblance to thoſe things now, it would be no leſs idle to trouble you with their nonſenſe than to believe it. We have indeed ſeen one thing that has amply repaid us for the trouble we have taken. It is the repreſentation of a boar-hunting in alto relievo, on white marble; and is at leaſt equal, if not ſuperior, to any thing of the kind I have met with in Italy. It conſiſts of four different parts, which form the hiſtory of this remarkable chace and its conſequences.

The firſt is the preparation for the hunt. There are twelve hunters, with each his lance, and a ſhort hanger under his left arm of a very ſingular form. The dogs reſemble thoſe we call lurchers. The horſes are done with great fire and ſpirit, and are perhaps a better proof of the excellence of the race, than even the teſtimony of their authors; for the artiſt that formed theſe muſt certainly have been accuſtomed to ſee very fine horſes.

The ſecond piece repreſents the chace.—The third, the death of the king, by a fall from his horſe.—And the fourth, the deſpair of the queen and her attendants, on receiving the news. She is repreſented as falling down in a ſwoon, and ſupported by her women, who are all in tears.

It

It is executed in the most masterly stile, and is indeed one of the finest remains of antiquity. It is preserved in the great church, which is noted through all Sicily for a remarkable echo; something in the manner of our whispering gallery at St. Paul's, though more difficult to be accounted for.

If one person stands at the west gate, and another places himself on the cornice, at the most distant point of the church, exactly behind the great altar, they can hold a conversation in very low whispers.

For many years this singularity was little known; and several of the confessing chairs being placed near the great altar, the wags, who were in the secret, used to take their station at the door of the cathedral; and by this means heard distinctly every word that passed betwixt the confessor and his penitent; of which, you may believe, they did

did not fail to make their own uſe when occaſion offered.—The moſt ſecret intrigues were diſcovered; and every woman in Agrigentum changed either her gallant or her confeſſor. Yet ſtill it was the ſame.—At laſt, however, the cauſe was found out; the chairs were removed, and other precautions were taken, to prevent the diſcovery of theſe ſacred myſteries; and a mutual amneſty paſſed amongſt all the offended parties.

Agrigentum, like Syracuſe, was long ſubject to the yoke of tyrants. Fazzello gives ſome account of their cruelty, but I have no intention of repeating it: One ſtory, however pleaſed me; it is a well known one, but as it is ſhort, you ſhall have it.

Perillo, a goldſmith, by way of paying court to Phalaris the tyrant, made him a preſent of a brazen bull, of admirable workmanſhip; hollow within, and ſo contrived that the voice of a perſon ſhut up in it, ſounded exactly like the bellowing of a real bull. The artiſt pointed out to the tyrant what an admirable effect this muſt produce, were he only to ſhut up a few criminals in it, and make a fire under them.

Phalaris, ſtruck with ſo horrid an idea, and perhaps curious to try the experiment, told the goldſmith that he himſelf was the only perſon worthy of animating his bull: that he muſt have ſtudied the note that made it roar to the greateſt advantage, and that it would be unjuſt to deprive him of any part of the honour of his invention. Upon which he ordered the goldſmith to be ſhut up, and made a great fire around the bull; which immediately began to roar, to the admiration and delight of all Agrigentum. Cicero ſays this bull was carried to Carthage at the taking of Agrigentum; and

was

was reſtored again by Scipio, after the deſtruction of that city.

Fazzello adds another ſtory, which is ſtill more to the honour of Phalaris. Two friends, Melanippus and Cariton, had conſpired his death. Cariton, in hopes of ſaving his friend from the danger of the enterprize, determined to execute it alone. However, in his attempt to poignard the tyrant, he was ſeized by the guards, and immediately put to the torture, to make him confeſs his accomplice: this he bore with the utmoſt fortitude, refuſing to make the diſcovery; 'till Melanippus, informed of the ſituation of his friend, ran to the tyrant, aſſuring him that he alone was the guilty perſon; that it was entirely by his inſtigation that Cariton had acted; and begged that he might be put on the rack in the place of his friend. Phalaris, ſtruck with ſuch heroiſm, pardoned them both.

Notwithſtanding this generous action, he was in many reſpects a barbarous tyrant. Fazzello gives the following account of his death, with which I ſhall conclude this letter, for I am monſtrouſly tired, and, I dare ſay, ſo are you. Zeno, the philoſopher, came to Agrigentum, and being admitted into the preſence of the tyrant, adviſed him, for his own comfort, as well as that of his ſubjects, to reſign his power, and to lead a private life. Phalaris did not reliſh theſe philoſophical ſentiments; and ſuſpecting Zeno to be in a conſpiracy with ſome of his ſubjects, ordered him to be put to the torture in preſence of the citizens of Agrigentum.

Zeno immediately began to reproach them with cowardice and puſilanimity in ſubmitting tamely to the yoke of ſo worthleſs a tyrant; and in a ſhort time raiſed ſuch a flame that they defeated the guards, and ſtoned Phalaris to death.—I dare ſay you

are

are glad they did it ſo quickly.—Well, I ſhall not write ſuch long letters for the future; for I aſſure you it is at leaſt as troubleſome to the writer as the reader. Adieu. We ſhall ſail to-morrow or next morning for Trapani, from whence you may expect to hear from me. We are now going out to examine more antique walls, but I ſhall not trouble you with them.

Farewell.

## LETTER XX.

June 16th.

WHEN I have nothing elſe to do, I generally take up the pen. We are now on the top of a high mountain, about half way betwixt Agrigentum and Palermo. Our ſea expedition by Trapani has failed, and we are determined to put no more confidence in that element, happy beyond meaſure to find ourſelves at a diſtance from it, though in the moſt wretched of villages. We have travelled all night on mules; and arrived here about ten o'clock, overcome with ſleep and fatigue. We have juſt had an excellent diſh of tea, which never fails to cure me of both; and I am now as freſh as when we ſet out. It has not had the ſame effect on my companions: they have thrown themſelves down on a vile ſtraw-

bed

bed in the corner of the hovel; and, in ſpite of a parcel of ſtarved chickens, that are fluttering about and picking the ſtraws all round them, they are already faſt aſleep.

I ſhall ſeize that time to recapitulate what has happened ſince my laſt.

The day after I wrote you, we made ſome little excurſions round Agrigentum. The country is delightful; producing corn, wine, and oil, in the greateſt abundance: the fields are, at the ſame time, covered with a variety of the fineſt fruits; oranges, lemons, pomegranates, almonds, piſtachio-nuts, *&c.* Theſe afforded us almoſt as agreeable an entertainment as the conſideration of the ruins from whence they ſpring.

We dined with the biſhop, according to agreement, and roſe from table, convinced that the antient Agrigentini could not poſſibly underſtand the true luxury of eating better than their deſcendants, to whom they have tranſmitted a very competent portion both of their ſocial virtues and vices. I beg their pardon for calling them vices, I wiſh I had a ſofter name for it; it looks like ingratitude for their hoſpitality, for which we owe them ſo much.

We were juſt thirty at table, but, upon my word, I do not think we had leſs than an hundred diſhes of meat. Theſe were dreſſed with the richeſt and moſt delicate ſauces; and convinced us that the old Roman proverb of "Siculus coquus et Sicula menſa," was not more applicable in their time, than it is at preſent. Nothing was wanting that could be invented to ſtimulate and to flatter the palate; and to create a falſe appetite as well as to ſatisfy it. Some of the very diſhes ſo much reliſhed by the Roman epicures made a part of the feaſt; particularly the morene, which is ſo often mentioned by their authors: it is a ſpecies of eel, found only in this part of the Mediterranean, and ſent from hence to ſeveral of the courts of Europe. It is not ſo fat and luſcious as other eels, ſo that you can eat a good deal more of it: its fleſh is as white as ſnow, and is indeed a very great delicacy. But a modern refinement in luxury has, I think, ſtill produced a greater: By a particular kind of management they make the livers of their fowls grow to a large ſize, and at the ſame time acquire a high and rich flavour. It is indeed a moſt incomparable diſh; but the means of procuring it is ſo cruel, that I will not even truſt it with you. Perhaps, without any bad intention, you might mention it to ſome of your friends, they to others, till at laſt it might come into the hands of thoſe that would be glad to try the experiment; and the whole race of poultry might ever have reaſon to curſe me: let it ſuffice to ſay, that it occaſions a painful and lingering death to the poor animal: that I know is enough to make you wish never to taste of it, whatever effect it may have upon others.

The Sicilians eat of every thing, and attempted to make us do the same. The company was remarkably merry, and did by no means belie their antient character, for most of them were more than half seas over, long before we rose from table; and I was somewhat apprehensive of a second edition of the Triremes scene, as they were beginning to reel exceedingly. By the bye, I do not doubt but that phrase of *Half seas over*, may have taken its origin from some such story. They begged us to make a bowl of punch, a liquor they had often heard of, but had never seen. The materials were immediately found, and we succeeded so well, that they preferred it to all the wines on the table, of which they had a great variety. We were obliged to

replenish

replenish the bowl so often, that I really expected to see most of them under the table. They called it Pontio, and spoke loudly in its praise; declaring, that Pontio (alluding to Pontius Pilate) was a much better fellow than they had ever taken him for. However, after dinner, one of them, a reverend canon, grew excessively sick, and while he was throwing up, he turned to me with a rueful countenance, and shaking his head, he groaned out, "Ah, Signor Capitano, sapeva sempre che Pontio era un grande traditore."—"I always knew that Pontius was a great traitor." Another of them overhearing him, exclaimed—"Aspettatevi Signor Canonico."—"Not so fast (said he) my good Canon."—"Niente al pregiudizio di Signor Pontio, vi prego.—Recordate, che Pontio v'ha fatto un canonico;—et Pontio ha fatto sua eccellenza uno Vescovo—Non scordatevi mai di vostri amici."

Now what do you think of theſe reverend fathers of the church? their merit, you will eaſily perceive, does not conſiſt in faſting and prayer.—Their creed, they ſay, they have a good deal modernized, and is much ſimpler than that of Athanaſius.—One of them told me, that if we would but ſtay with them for ſome little time, we ſhould ſoon be convinced that they were the happieſt fellows on earth. "We have exploded (ſaid he) from our ſyſtem every thing that is diſmal or melancholy; and are perſuaded, that of all the roads in the univerſe, the road to heaven muſt be the pleaſanteſt and leaſt gloomy: If it be not ſo, (added he) God have mercy upon us, for I am afraid we ſhall never get there." I told him I could not flatter him; "That if laughing was really a ſin, as ſome people taught, they were certainly the greateſt of all ſinners." "Well (ſaid he) we ſhall at leaſt endeavour to be happy here; and that, I am perſuaded, is the beſt of all preparations

rations for happineſs hereafter. Abſtinence (continued he) from all innocent and lawful pleaſures, we reckon one of the greateſt ſins, and guard againſt it with the utmoſt care: and I am pretty ſure it is a ſin that none of us here will ever be damned for."—He concluded by repeating two lines, which he told me was their favourite maxim; the meaning of which was exactly thoſe of Mr. Pope,

"For God is paid when man receives,
"To enjoy is to obey."

This is not the firſt time I have met with this libertine ſpirit amongſt the Roman Catholic clergy. There is ſo much nonſenſe and mummery in their worſhip, that they are afraid leſt ſtrangers ſhould believe they are ſerious; and perhaps too often fly to the oppoſite extreme.

We were, however, much pleaſed with the biſhop; he is greatly and deſervedly reſpected,

ſpected, yet his preſence did no wiſe diminiſh, but rather increaſed, the jollity of the company. He entered into every joke, joined in the repartee, at which he is a great proficient, and entirely laid aſide his epiſcopal dignity; which, however, I am told, he knows very well how to aſſume when it is neceſſary. He placed us next to himſelf, and behaved indeed, in every reſpect, with the greateſt eaſe and politeneſs. He is of one of the firſt families of the iſland, and brother to the Prince of ——. I had his whole pedigree pat, but now I have loſt it; no matter: he is an honeſt, pleaſant, little fellow, and that is of much more conſequence. He is not yet forty; and ſo high a promotion in ſo early a period of life, is reckoned very extraordinary, this being the richeſt biſhoprick in the kingdom. He is a good ſcholar, and very deeply read, both in ancient and modern learning; and his genius is in no degree inferior to his erudition. The ſimilarity

larity of character and circumſtances ſtruck me ſo ſtrongly, that I could ſcarce help thinking I had got beſide our worthy and reſpectable friend, the b——p of D——y, which, I aſſure you, ſtill added greatly to the pleaſure I had in his company. I told the biſhop of this; adding, that he was brother to l—d B——l: he ſeemed much pleaſed, and ſaid, he had often heard of the family, both when lord B—— was ambaſſador in Spain, and his other brother commander in the Mediterranean.

We found in this company a number of Free Maſons, who were delighted beyond meaſure, when they diſcovered that we were their brethren. They preſſed us to ſpend a few more days amongſt them, and offered us letters to Palermo, and every other town we ſhould think of viſiting; but the heats are increaſing ſo violently, that we were afraid of prolonging our expedition, leſt we ſhould be caught by the

Sirocc

Sirocc winds, ſuppoſed to blow from the burning deſarts of Africa, and ſometimes attended with dangerous conſequences to thoſe that travel over Sicily.

But I find I have omitted ſeveral circumſtances of our dinner. I ſhould have told you, that it was an annual feaſt given by the nobility of Agrigentum to the biſhop. It was ſerved in an immenſe granary, half full of wheat, on the ſea ſhore, choſen on purpoſe to avoid the heat. The whole was on plate: and what appeared ſingular to us, but I believe is a much better method than ours; great part of the fruit was ſerved up with the ſecond courſe, the firſt diſh of which that went round was ſtrawberries. The Sicilians were a good deal ſurpriſed to ſee us eat them with cream and ſugar, yet upon trial they did not at all diſlike the compoſition.

The deſert conſiſted of a great variety of fruits, and ſtill a greater of ices: theſe were ſo diſguiſed in the ſhapes of peaches, figs, oranges, nuts, &c. that a perſon unaccuſtomed to ices might very eaſily have been taken in, as an honeſt ſea officer was lately at the houſe of a certain miniſter of your acquaintance, not leſs diſtinguiſhed for the elegance of his table, than the exact formality and ſubordination to be obſerved at it. After the ſecond courſe was removed; and the ices, in the ſhape of various fruits and ſweetmeats, advanced by way of rear-guard; one of the ſervants carried the figure of a fine large peach to the captain, who, unacquainted with deceit of any kind, never doubted that it was a real one; and cutting it through the middle, in a moment had one large half of it in his mouth; at firſt he only looked grave, and blew up his cheeks to give it more room; but the violence of the cold ſoon getting the better of his patience, he began to tumble it about from ſide to ſide in his mouth, his eyes ruſhing out of water, till at laſt, able to hold

no

no longer, he spit it out upon his plate, exclaiming with a horrid oath, "A painted snowball, by G—!" and wiping away his tears with his napkin, he turned in a rage to the Italian servant that had helped him, with a "d—n your maccaroni eyes, you son of a b—, what did you mean by that?" —The fellow, who did not understand a word of it, could not forbear smiling, which still convinced the captain the more that it was a trick; and he was just going to throw the rest of the snowball in his face, but was prevented by one of the company; when recovering from his passion, and thinking the object unworthy of it, he only added in a softer tone, "Very well, neighbour, I only wish I had you on board ship for half an hour, you should have a dozen before you could say Jack Robinson, for all your painted cheeks."

I ask pardon for this digression, but as it is a good laughable story, I know you will

will excuſe it. About ſix o'clock, we took a cordial leave of our jolly friends at Agrigentum; and embarked on board our Sparonaro at the new port. I ſhould have told you, that this harbour has lately been made at a very great expence; this city having always been one of the principal ports of the iſland, for the exportation of grain. The biſhop and his company went into a large barge, and ſailed round the harbour, we ſaluted them as we went out; they returned the compliment, and we took a ſecond leave. The evening was fine, and we coaſted along for a good many miles; we paſſed ſeveral points and little promontories, that were exceedingly beautiful and pictureſque, many of them were covered with noble large aloes in full blow. In one place, I counted upwards of 200 of thoſe fine majeſtic plants all in flower; a ſight which I imagined was hardly to be met with in the world.—After ſun-ſet,—alas, fain would I conceal what happened after ſun-ſet! —but life you know is chequered with good and evil, and it would have been great preſumption to receive ſo much of the one, without expecting a little daſh of the other too.—Beſides, a ſea expedition is nothing without a ſtorm. Our journal would never have been readable, had it not been for this.—Well I aſſure you, we had it. It was not indeed ſo violent as the great one off Louiſburgh, or perhaps even that deſcribed by Virgil; the reading of which is ſaid to have made people ſea-ſick; but it was rather too much for our little bark.—I was going to tell you that after ſun-ſet the ſky began to overcaſt, and in a ſhort time, the whole atmoſphere appeared firey and threatening. We attempted to get into ſome creek, but could find none. The wind grew loud, and we found it was in vain to proceed; but as the night was dark and hazy, we were dubious about the poſſibility of reaching the port of Agrigentum.

How-

However, this was all we had for it, as there were none other within many miles. Accordingly we tacked about, and plying both oars and ſail, with great care not to come amongſt the rocks and breakers, in about two hours we ſpied the light-houſe; by which we directed our courſe, and got ſafely into port, betwixt one and two in the morning: we lay down on our mattraſs, and ſlept ſound till ten, when finding the falſity of our hypotheſis, that there could be no bad weather in the Mediterranean at this ſeaſon, we unanimouſly agreed to have nothing more to do with Sparonaros, and ſent immediately to engage mules to carry us over the mountains to Palermo. The ſtorm continued with violence the whole day, and made us often thank heaven that we had got ſafely back. It was not till five in the afternoon that we had mules, guides, and guards provided us; when we ſet off, pretty much in the ſame order, and in the ſame equipage as we had done about three weeks ago from Meſſina. Our guards attempted to fill us with the moſt dreadful apprehenſions of this road, ſhewing us every mile, where ſuch a one was robbed, ſuch another was murdered; and entertained us with ſuch melancholy ditties the greateſt part of the way. Indeed, if one half of their ſtories be true, it is certainly the moſt dangerous road in the world; but I looked upon moſt of them as fictions, invented only to increaſe their own conſequence, and to procure a little more money. There is, indeed, ſome foundation for theſe ſtories; as there are numbers of gibbets erected on the road *in terrorem*; and every little baron has the power of life and death in his own domain. Our biſhop's brother, whoſe name I have forgot, ſeized lately four and twenty of thoſe deſperate banditti, after a ſtout reſiſtance, where ſeveral were killed on both ſides; and notwithſtanding that ſome of them were under the protection of the nobility, and in their

 ſervice,

ſervice, they were all hanged. However, this has by no means rooted them out. Our guards in the ſuſpicious places went with their pieces cock'd, and kept a cloſe look-out to either ſide of them; but we ſaw nothing to alarm us, except the moſt dreadful roads in the world; in many places worſe than any thing I ever met with amongſt the Alps.

After travelling about twenty miles, we arrived by two in the morning at the moſt wretched—I don't know what to call it—there was not any one thing to be had but a little ſtraw for the mules. However, after a good deal of difficulty, we at laſt got fire enough to boil our tea-kettle, and having brought bread from Agrigentum, we made an excellent meal. Our tea-table was a round ſtone in the field, and as the moon ſhone bright, we had no occaſion for any other luminary. You may believe our ſtay here was as ſhort as poſſible; the houſe was too dreadfully naſty to enter it, and the ſtable was full of poor wretches ſleeping on the bare ground. In ſhort, I never ſaw in any country ſo miſerable an Inn, for ſo it is ſtiled. We mounted our cavalry with all expedition, and in a very ſhort time got into the woods, where we we were ſerenaded by the nightingale as we went along, who made us a full apology and atonement for the bad cheer we had met with. In a ſhort time it was day, and then we had entertainment enough from the varied ſcenes of the moſt beautiful, wild and romantic country in the world.—The fertility of many of the plains is truly aſtoniſhing, without incloſures, without manure, and almoſt without culture. It is with reaſon, that this Iſland was ſtiled "Romani imperii horreum," the granary of the Roman empire. Were it cultivated, it would ſtill be the great granary of Europe. Pliny ſays it yielded a hundred after one; and Diodorus, who was a native of the

iſland,

iſland, and wrote on the ſpot, aſſures us that it produced wheat and other grain ſpontaneouſly; and Homer advances the ſame fact in the Odyſſey:

The ſoil untill'd a ready harveſt yields,
With wheat and barley wave the golden fields;
Spontaneous wines from weighty cluſters pour,
And Jove deſcends in each prolific ſhower.

POPE.

Many of the mountains ſeem to be formed by ſubterraneous fire; ſeveral of them retain their conical figure and their craters, but not ſo exact as thoſe on Mount Ætna, as they are probably much older. I likewiſe obſerved many pieces of lava on the road, and in the beds of the torrents; and a good deal of the ſtone called tufa, which is certainly the production of a volcano; ſo that I have no doubt, that a great part of this iſland, as well as the neighbouring ones of Lipari, &c. has been originally formed by ſubterraneous fire: we like-while passed some quarries of a kind of talc; and also of a coarse alabaster; of this they make a sort of stucco or plaister, resembling that of Paris; but what I much regretted, we missed seeing the famous salt of Agrigentum; found in the earth, about four or five miles from that city. It has this remarkable property different from all other salt, that in the fire it presently melts; but in the water it cracks and splits but never dissolves. It is celebrated by Pliny, Aristotle, and others of the antient, as well as modern naturalists. Fazzello, whom I have brought along with me to read by the road, says, he has often experienced this; he adds from the authority of these antient authors, that they formerly had mines of this salt, so pure and solid, that the statuaries and sculptors preferred it to marble, and made various works of it.

The poor people of the village have found us out, and with looks full of misery

have

have surrounded our door.—Accursed tyranny,—what despicable objects we become in thy hands!—Is it not inconceivable, how any government should be able to render poor and wretched, a country which produces almost spontaneously, every thing that even luxury can desire? But alas! poverty and wretchedness have ever attended the Spanish yoke, both on this, and on t'other side of the globe.—They make it their boast, that the sun never sets on their dominions, but forget that since they became such, they have left him nothing to see in his course but deserted fields, barren wildernesses, oppressed peasants, and lazy, lying, lecherous monks.—Such are the fruits of their boasted conquests.—They ought rather to be ashamed that ever the sun should see them at all.—The sight of these poor people has filled me with indignation. This village is surrounded by the finest country in the world, yet there was neither bread nor wine to be found in it,

and

and the poor inhabitants appear more than half ſtarved.

"'Mongſt Ceres' richeſt gifts with want oppreſs'd,
"And 'midſt the flowing vineyard, die of thirſt.

I ſhall now think of concluding, as I do not recollect that I have much more to ſay to you. Beſides, I find myſelf exceeding ſleepy. I ſincerely wiſh it may not be the ſame caſe with you, before you have read thus far. We have ordered our mules to be ready by five o'clock, and ſhall again travel all night;—the heats are too great to allow of it by day; adieu.—Theſe two fellows are ſtill ſound aſleep. In a few minutes I ſhall be ſo too, for the pen is almoſt dropping out of my hand. Farewell.

## LETTER XXI.

Palermo, June 19.

WE are now arrived at the great capital of Sicily, which in our opinion in beauty and elegance is greatly ſuperior to Naples. It is not, indeed, ſo large, but the regularity, the uniformity and neatneſs of its ſtreets and buildings, render it much more pleaſing; it is full of people, who have moſtly an air of affluence and gaiety. And indeed we ſeem to have got into a new world.—But ſtop—not ſo faſt.—I had forgot that you have ſtill 50 miles to travel on a curſed ſtubborn mule, over rocks and precipices; for I can ſee no reaſon, why we ſhould bring you at once into all the ſweets of Palermo, without bearing at leaſt ſome little part in the

the fatigues of the journey. Come, we ſhall make them as ſhort as poſſible.

We left you, I think, in a little village on the top of a high mountain. We ſhould indeed uſe you very ill, were we to leave you there any longer; for I own it is the very worſt country quarter, that ever fell to my lot. However, we got a good comfortable ſleep in it, the only one thing it afforded us; and the fleas, the bugs, and chickens, did all that lay in their power even to deprive us of that, but we defied them. Our two leaders came to awake us before five, apoſtrophy-ing their entry with a detail of the horrid robberies and murders that had been com-mitted in the neighbourhood; all of them, you may be ſure, on the very road that we were to go.

Our whole ſquadron was drawn out, and we were ranged in order of battle, by five

five o'clock, when we began our march, attended by the whole village, man, woman, and child. We ſoon got down amongſt the woods, and endeavoured to forget the objects of miſery we had left behind us. The beauty and richneſs of the country increaſed in proportion as we advanced. The mountains, although of a great height (that we have left is near 4000 feet, the mercury ſtanding at 26 inches 2 lines) are covered to the very ſummit with the richeſt paſture. The graſs in the valleys is already burnt up, ſo that the flocks are all upon the mountains. The gradual ſeparation of heat and cold, is very viſible in taking a view of them. The valleys are brown and ſcorched, and ſo are the mountains to a conſiderable height; they then begin to take a ſhade of green, which grows deeper and deeper, and covers the whole upper region; however, on the ſummit, the graſs and corn are by no means ſo luxuriant as about the middle.

We

We were amazed at the richneſs of the crops, far ſuperior to any thing I had ever ſeen either in England or Flanders, where the happy ſoil is aſſiſted by all the arts of cultivation; whilſt here, the wretched huſbandman can hardly afford to give it a furrow; and gathers in with a heavy heart, the moſt luxuriant harveſt. To what purpoſe is it given him? only to lie a dead weight upon his hand, ſometimes till it is entirely loſt; exportation being prohibited to all ſuch as cannot pay exorbitantly for it to the ſovereign.—What a contraſt is there betwixt this, and the little uncouth country of Switzerland!—to be ſure, the dreadful conſequences of oppreſſion can never be ſet in a more ſtriking oppoſition to the bleſſings and charms of liberty. Switzerland, the very excreſcence of Europe, where nature ſeems to have thrown out all her cold and ſtagnating humours; full of lakes, marſhes, and woods, and ſurrounded by immenſe rocks, and

and everlasting mountains of ice, the barren, but sacred, ramparts of liberty. Switzerland, enjoying every blessing, where every blessing seems to have been denied; whilst Sicily, covered by the most luxuriant hand of Nature; where Heaven seems to have showered down its richest blessings with the utmost prodigality; groans under the most abject poverty, and with a pale and wan visage, starves in the midst of plenty.—It is liberty alone that works this standing miracle.—Under her plastic hands the mountains sink, the lakes are drained; and these rocks, these marshes, these woods, become so many sources of wealth and of pleasure.—But what has temperance to do with wealth?

"Here reigns Content,
"And Nature's child Simplicity; long since
"Exil'd from polished realms."

"'Tis Industry supplies
"The little Temperance wants; and rosy Health
"Sits smiling at the board."

You will begin to think I am in danger of turning poetical in these classic fields;— I am sure I neither suspected any of the mountains we have passed to be Parnassus; nor did I believe any one of the nine foolish enough to inhabit them, except Melpomenè perhaps, as she is so fond of tragical faces: however, I shall now get you out of them as soon as possible, and bring you once more into the gay world. I assure you, I have often wished that you could have lent me your muse, on this expedition; my letters would then have been more worth the reading; but you must take the will for the deed.

After travelling till about midnight, we arrived at another miserable village, where we slept for some hours on straw, and continued our journey again by day-break. We had the pleasure of seeing the rising sun from the top of a pretty high mountain, and were delighted with the prospect

of

of Strombolo, and the other Lipari Islands, at a great distance from us. On our descent from this mountain, we found ourselves on the banks of the sea, and took that road, preferable to an inland one, although several miles nearer. We soon lighted from our mules, and plunged into the water, which has ever made one of our greatest pleasures in this expedition: nobody that has not tried it, can conceive the delight of this; after the fatigue of such a journey, and passing three days without undressing. Your friend Fullarton, though only seventeen, but whose mind and body now equally despise every fatigue, found himself strong as a lion, and fit to begin such another march. We boiled our tea-kettle under a fig-tree, and eat a breakfast that might have served a company of strolling players.

The approach to Palermo is fine. The alleys are planted with fruit-trees, and large American aloes in full blow.—Near

 the

the city we paſſed a place of execution, where the quarters of a number of robbers were hung up upon hooks, like ſo many hams; ſome of them appeared newly executed, and made a very unſightly figure. On our arrival, we learned that a prieſt and three others had been taken a few days ago, after an obſtinate defence, in which ſeveral were killed on both ſides; the prieſt, rather than ſubmit to his conquerors, plunged his hanger into his breaſt, and died on the ſpot: the reſt ſubmitted and were executed.

As there is but one inn in Palermo, we were obliged to agree to their own terms (five ducats a day). We are but indifferently lodged; however, it is the only inn we have yet ſeen in Sicily, and indeed, may be ſaid to be the only one in the iſland. It is kept by a noiſy troubleſome Frenchwoman, who I find will plague us; there is no keeping her out of our rooms, and

ſhe

ſhe never comes in without telling us of ſuch a prince and ſuch a duke, that were ſo ſuperlatively happy at being lodged in her houſe: we can eaſily learn that they were all deſperately in love with her; and indeed ſhe ſeems to take it very much amiſs, that we are not inclined to be of the ſame ſentiments. I have already been obliged to tell her, that we are very retired ſort of people, and do not like company; I find ſhe does not eſteem us the better for it; and this morning, (as I paſſed through the kitchen, without ſpeaking to her) I overheard her exclaim, "Ah mon Dieu! comme ces Anglois ſont "ſauvages." I believe we muſt take more notice of her, otherwiſe we ſhall certainly have our rent raiſed; but ſhe is as fat as a pig, and as ugly as a devil, and lays on a quantity of paint on each of her ſwelled cheeks, that looks like a great plaiſter of red Morocco. Her picture is hanging in the room where I am now writing, as well as that of her husband, who, by the bye, is a ninny: they are no less vile curiosities than the originals.—He is drawn with his snuff-box open in one hand, and a dish of coffee in the other; and at the same time, *fait l'aimable à Madame.* I took notice of this triple occupation, which seemed to imply something particular. She told me that the thought was her's; that her husband was exceedingly fond of snuff and of coffee, and wanted by this to shew that he was still more occupied with her than with either of them.—I could not help applauding the ingenuity of the conceit. Madame is painted with an immense bouquet in her breast, and an orange in her right-hand, emblematic of her sweetness and purity; and has the prettiest little smirk on her face you can imagine. She told me that she insisted on the painter drawing her *avec le souris sur le visage*, but as he had not *esprit* enough to make her smile naturally, she was obliged to

force

force one, "qui n'etoit pas tout a fait "si jolie que le naturel, mais qui vaudroit "toujours mieux que de parroitre ſombre." I agreed with her perfectly; and aſſured her it became her very much, "pareeque "les dames graſſes ſont toujours de bonne "humeur."—I found, however, that ſhe would willingly have excuſed me the latter part of the compliment, which more than loſt all that I had gained by the former. "Il eſt vrai" (ſaid ſhe, a good deal piqued) "j'ai un peu de l'em bon point, mais pas "tant graſſe pourtant." I pretended to excuſe myſelf, from not underſtanding all the fineſſe of the language; and aſſured her, that *de l'em bon point* was the very phraſe I meant to make uſe of. She accepted the apology, and we are again reconciled; for, to give the devil his due, they are good-humoured. She made me a curtſey, and repeated, "Oui, Monſieur, "pour parler comme il faut; il faut dire "*de l'em bon point.*—On ne dit pas grasse."* I assured her, bowing to the ground, that the word should for ever be razed from my vocabulary. She left me with a gracious smile, and a curtsey much lower than the first; adding, "Je sçavois bien que Mon-"sieur etoit un homme comme il faut;" at the same time tripping off on her tip-toes, as light as a feather, to shew me how much I had been mistaken. This woman made me recollect (what I have always observed) how little the manners of the French are to be changed by their connection with other nations; allowing none to be in any degree worthy of imitation but their own. Although she has now been here these twenty years, she is still as perfectly French, as if she had never been without the gates of Paris; and looks upon every woman in Palermo with the utmost contempt, because they have never seen that capital, nor heard

the

the ſublime muſick of its opera. She is likewiſe (allowing for the difference of rank) an admirable epitome of all French women, whoſe univerſal paſſion has ever been the deſire of admiration, and of appearing young; and ever would be, I believe, were they to live to the age of a thouſand. Any perſon that will take a look of the withered death's heads in their publick places, covered over with a thick maſk of paint, will be convinced of this.—Now, our old ladies, when they get to the wrong ſide of ſixty, generally take a jump up to the borders of fourſcore, and appear no leſs vain of their years, than ever they were of their youth. I know ſome of them, that I am ſure are not leſs happy, nor leſs contented, nor (I might almoſt add) leſs admired with their wrinkles, than ever they were with their dimples. I do not know whether a cheerful old woman, who is willing to appear ſo, is more reſpectable,

 or

or more estimable; or a withered witch, who fills up every wrinkle with varnish, and at fourscore attempts to give herself the bloom of four-and-twenty, is ridiculous and contemptible:—but as dinner is on the table, I shall leave it to you to determine. Adieu.

## LETTER XXII.

Palermo, June 23d.

I SHALL have a great deal to write you about this city; we are every day more delighted with it, and ſhall leave it with much regret. We have now delivered our letters, in conſequence of which we are loaded with civilities, and have got into a very agreeable ſet of acquaintance.—But I ſhall firſt attempt to give you ſome little idea of the town, and then ſpeak of its inhabitants. It is by much the moſt regular I have ſeen, and is built upon that plan, which I think all large cities ought to follow. The two great ſtreets interſect each other in the center of the city, where they form a handſome ſquare, called the Ottangolo, adorned with elegant uniform buildings. From the center of this ſquare, you ſee the whole of theſe noble ſtreets, and the four great gates of the city which terminate them; the ſymmetry and beauty of which produce a fine effect. The whole of theſe are to be magnificently illuminated ſome time next month, and muſt certainly be the fineſt ſight in the world. The four gates are each at the diſtance of about half a mile, (the diameter of the city being no more than a mile:) theſe are elegant pieces of architecture richly adorned; particularly the *Porta Nova* and *Porta Felice*, terminating the great ſtreet called the *Corſo*, that runs ſouth weſt and north eaſt. The leſſer ſtreets in general run parallel to theſe great ones; ſo that from every part of the city, in a few minutes walking, you are ſure to arrive at one of the capital ſtreets. The *Porta Felice* (by much the handſomeſt of the gates) opens to the *Marino*, a delightful walk, which conſtitutes one of the great pleaſures of the nobility of Palermo.

It

It is bounded on one ſide by the wall of the city, and on the other by the ſea, from whence, even at this ſcorching ſeaſon, there is always an agreeable breeze. In the center of the Marino they have lately erected an elegant kind of temple, which, during the ſummer months, is made uſe of as an orcheſtra for muſick; and as in this ſeaſon they are obliged to convert the night into day, the concert does not begin till the clock ſtrikes midnight, which is the ſignal for the ſymphony to ſtrike up: at that time the walk is crowded with carriages and people on foot; and the better to favour pleaſure and intrigue, there is an order, that no perſon, of whatever quality, ſhall preſume to carry a light with him. The flambeaux are extinguiſhed at the Porta Felice, where the ſervants wait for the return of the carriages; and the company generally continue an hour or two together in utter darkneſs; except when the intruding moon, with her horns and

and her chaſtity, comes to diſturb them. The concert finiſhes about two in the morning, when, for the moſt part, every huſband goes home to his own wife. This is an admirable inſtitution, and never produces any ſcandal: no huſband is ſuch a brute as to deny his wife the Marino; and the ladies are ſo cautious and circumſpect on their ſide, that the more to avoid giving offence, they very often put on maſques.

Their other amuſements conſiſt chiefly in their *Converſaziones*, of which they have a variety every night. There is one general one, ſupported by the ſubſcription of the nobility, which is open every evening at ſun-ſet, and continues till midnight, when the Marino begins. It better deſerves the name of a converſation than any I have ſeen in Italy; for here the people really come to converſe, whereas in Italy, they only go to play at cards and eat ices. I

have

have obferved, that feldom or never one half of the company is engaged in play, nor do they either play long or deep. There are a number of apartments belonging to this converfation, illuminated with wax lights, and kept exceedingly cool and agreeable; and it is indeed altogether one of the moft fenfible and comfortable inftitutions I have feen: befides this, there are generally a number of particular converfations every night, and what will a good deal furprize you, thefe are always held in the apartments of the lying-in ladies; for in this happy climate, child-bearing is diverted of all its terrors, and is only confidered as a party of pleafure. This circumftance we were ignorant of till t'other morning. The duke of Verdura, who does us the honours of the place, with great attention and politenefs, came to tell us, we had a vifit to make, that was indifpenfable. "The Princefs Paterno

"(faid

" (ſaid he) was brought to bed laſt night; " and it is abſolutely incumbent on you " to pay your reſpects to her this even-" ing." At firſt I thought he was in joke, but he aſſured me he was ſerious, and that it would be looked upon as a great unpoliteneſs to neglect it.—Accordingly we went about ſun-ſet, and found the princeſs ſitting up in her bed, in an elegant undreſs, with a number of her friends around her. She talked as uſual, and ſeemed to be perfectly well. This converſation is repeated every night during her convaleſcence, which generally laſts for about eleven or twelve days. This cuſtom is univerſal, and as the ladies here are very prolific, there are for the moſt part three or four of theſe aſſemblies going on in the city at the ſame time; poſſibly the Marino may not a little contribute towards them.

The

The Sicilian ladies marry at thirteen or fourteen, and are ſometimes grandmothers before they are thirty.—The Count Stetela preſented us a few days ago to his couſin, the Princeſs Partana, who he told us had a great number of children, the eldeſt of which was a very fine girl of fifteen. We talked to the princeſs for half an hour, not in the leaſt doubting all the time that ſhe was the daughter, till at laſt the young lady came in; and even then, it was not eaſy to ſay which appeared the handſomeſt or the youngeſt. This lady has had twelve children, and is ſtill in her bloom; ſhe aſſured me that ſhe never enjoyed more perfect health than when ſhe was in child-bed;—that during the time of her pregnancy ſhe was often indiſpoſed, but that immediately on delivery ſhe was cured of all her complaints, and was capable of enjoying the company of her friends even more than at any other time. I expreſſed my ſurpriſe at this very ſingular happineſs of their cli-

mate

mate or conſtitutions; but ſhe appeared ſtill more ſurpriſed when I told her that we loſt many of our fineſt women in childbed, and that even the moſt fortunate and eaſy deliveries were attended with violent pain and anguiſh.—She lamented the fate of our ladies, and thanked Heaven that ſhe was born a Sicilian.

What this ſingularity is owing to, let the learned determine; but it is ſurely one of the capital bleſſings of theſe climates, where the curſe that was laid upon mother Eve ſeems to be entirely taken off: I don't know how the ladies here have deſerved this exemption, as they have at leaſt as much both of Eve and the ſerpent as ours have, and ſtill retain their appetite, as ſtrong as ever, for forbidden fruit.—It ſeems hard, that in our own country, and in Switzerland, where the women in general are the chaſteſt in Europe, that this curſe ſhould fall the heavieſt: it is probably owing to the

the climate:—In cold, but more particularly in mountainous countries, births are difficult and dangerous; in warm and low places they are more easy; the air of the first hardens and contracts the fibres, that of the second softens and relaxes them. In some places in Switzerland, and amongst the Alps, they lose almost one half of their women in childbed, and those that can afford it, often go down to the low countries some weeks before they lie in, and find their deliveries much easier. One may easily conceive what a change it must make upon the whole frame, to add the pressure of a column of air of two or three thousand feet more than it is accustomed to: and if muscular motion is performed by the pressure of the atmosphere, as some have alleged, how much must this add to the action of every muscle!—However, if this hypothesis were true, our strength should have been diminished one third on the top of Ætna, which did not appear to be the

 case;

caſe; as we had paſſed through one third of the quantity of air of the whole atmoſphere. I have often thought that phyſicians pay too little attention to theſe conſiderations; and that in ſkilful hands they might be turned to great account, in the cure of many diſeaſes: they only ſend their patients to ſuch a degree of latitude, but never think of the degree of altitude in the atmoſphere. Thus, people with the ſame complaints are ſent to Aix and to Marſeilles, although the air in theſe two places muſt be eſſentially different. Marſeilles is on the level of the ſea, and Aix (as I myſelf meaſured it) is near 600 feet above it.—Now I am perſuaded, that in ſuch a country as Switzerland, or on ſuch a mountain as Ætna, where it is eaſy at all times to take off a preſſure from the human body of many thouſand pounds weight, that an ingenious phyſician might make great diſcoveries; nor indeed would theſe diſcoveries be confined to the changing of the quantity of air that preſſes on the body, but would likewiſe be extended to the changing of the quality of the air we breathe; which, on the ſide of Ætna, or any very high mountain, is more varied than in travelling through fifty degrees of latitude. I beg pardon for this digreſſion; the only amends I can make, is to put it out of my power to trouble you with any more, and thus abruptly aſſure you how much, &c.

## LETTER XXIII.

Palermo, June 26th.

OUR fondneſs for Palermo increaſes every day, and we are beginning to look forward with regret to the time of our leaving it, which is now faſt approaching. We have made acquaintance with many ſenſible and agreeable people. The Sicilians appear frank and ſincere; and their politeneſs does not conſiſt in ſhew and grimace, like ſome of the polite nations of the continent. The viceroy ſets the pattern of hoſpitality, and he is followed by the reſt of the nobles. He is an amiable, agreeable man, and I believe is as much beloved and eſteemed as a viceroy to an abſolute monarch can be. He was in England in his youth, and is ſtill fond of many of our authors, with whom he ſeems to to be intimately acquainted; he ſpeaks the language tolerably well, and encourages the learning of it amongſt his people.—He may be conſidered with regard to Naples, as what the lord lieutenant of Ireland is with regard to England, with this trifling difference, that, like his maſter, he is inveſted with abſolute authority; and keeps his parliament (for he has one too) in the moſt perfect ſubjection. The patriots here, although a very numerous body, have never been able to gain one point, no nor a place, nor even a penſion for a needy friend. Had lord Townſhend the power of the marquis Fogliano, I ſuppoſe your Hibernian ſquabbles (of which we hear ſo much, even at this diſtant corner) would ſoon have an end.—Notwithſtanding this great authority, he is affable and familiar, and makes his houſe agreeable to every body. We go very often to his aſſemblies, and have dined with him ſeveral times; his table is ſerved with elegance and magnificence, much ſuperior indeed to that of his Sicilian majesty, who eats off a service of plate, at least 300 years old, very black and rusty indeed: I heard a gentleman ask one day, whilst we were standing round the table, if it had not been dug out of Herculaneum. That of the viceroy is very elegant, and indeed the whole of his entertainments correspond with it; though we have as yet seen nothing here, to be compared to the luxury of our feast in the granary at Agrigentum.

The Sicilian cookery is a mixture of the French and Spanish; and the Olio still preserves its rank and dignity in the center of the table, surrounded by a numerous train of fricassees, fricandeaus, ragouts, and pet de loups; like a grave Spanish Don, amidst a number of little smart marquis.—The other nobility, whom we have had occasion to see, are likewise very magnificent in their entertainments; but most particularly in in their deserts and ices, of which there is a greater variety than I have seen in any other country. They are very temperate with regard to wine; though, since we have taught them our method of toasting ladies they are fond of, and of hob and nobing with their friends, ringing the two glasses together; this social practice has animated them so much, that they have been sometimes led to drink a greater quantity than they are accustomed to; and they often reproach us with having made them drunkards. In their ordinary living they are very frugal and temperate; and from the sobriety we have seen here, we are now more persuaded that the elevated situation of Agrigentum must be one great cause of its drunkenness.

The Sicilians have always had the character of being very amorous, and surely not without reason. The whole nation are poets, even the peasants; and a man stands a poor chance for a miſtreſs, that is not capable of celebrating her praiſes. I believe, it is generally allowed that the paſtoral poetry had its origin in this iſland; and Theocritus, after whom they ſtill copy, will ever be looked upon as the prince of paſtoral poets. And indeed in muſick too, as well as poetry, the ſoft, amorous pieces are generally ſtiled *Siciliani*; theſe they uſed to play all night under their miſtreſſes' windows, to expreſs the delicacy of their paſſion; but ſerenading is not now ſo much in faſhion, as it was during the time of their more intimate connection with Spain, when it was ſaid by one of their authors, that no perſon could paſs for a man of gallantry that had not got a cold; and was ſure never to ſucceed in making love, unleſs he made it in a hoarſe voice. The ladies are not now ſo rigid, and will ſometimes condeſcend to hear a man, even although he ſhould ſpeak in a clear tone.—Neither do they any longer require the

prodigious

prodigious martial feats, that were then necessary to win them.—The attacking of a mad bull, or a wild boar, was reckoned the handsomest compliment a lover could pay to his mistress; and the putting these animals to death softened her heart much more than all the sighing love-sick tales that could be invented. This has been humorously ridiculed by one of their poets. He says that Cupid's little golden dart was now changed into a massy spear, which answered a double purpose; for at the same time that it pierced the tough bull's hide, it likewise pierced the tender lady's heart.—But these Gothick customs are now confined to Spain, and the gentle Sicilians have reassumed their softness. To tell you the truth, gallantry is pretty much upon the same footing here as in Italy, the establishment of Ciccisbees is pretty general, though not quite so universal as on the continent. However, a breach of the marriage vow is no longer looked upon as one of the deadly sins;

and

and the confeſſors fall upon eaſy and pleaſant enough methods of making them atone for it. The huſbands are content; and like able generals, make up for the loſs of one fortreſs, by the taking of another. However, female licentiouſneſs has by no means come to ſuch a height as in Italy. We have ſeen a great deal of domeſtic happineſs; huſbands and wives that truly love one another, and whoſe mutual care and pleaſure is the education of their children. I could name a number;—The Duke of Verdura, the Prince Partana, the Count Buſcemi, and many others who live in the moſt ſacred union. Such ſights are very rare on the continent. But indeed the ſtile that young people are brought up in here, ſeems to lay a much more ſolid foundation for matrimonial happineſs, than either in France or Italy. The young ladies are not ſhut up in convents till the day of their marriage, but for the moſt part live in the houſe with their parents, where

they

they receive their education, and are every day in company with their friends and relations. From what I can observe, I think they are allowed almost as much liberty as with us. In their great assemblies, we often see a club of young people (of both sexes) get together in a corner, and amuse themselves for hours, at cross purposes or such like games, without the mothers being under the least anxiety; indeed, we sometimes join in these little parties, and find them extremely entertaining. In general, they are quick and lively, and have a number of those *jeux d'esprit*, which I think must ever be a proof, in all countries, of the familiar intercourse betwixt the young people of the two sexes; for all these games are insipid, if they are not seasoned by something of that invisible and subtile agency, which renders every thing more interesting in these mixed societies, than in the lifeless ones, composed of only one part of the species. Thus, in Italy,

Spain, and Portugal, I have never ſeen any of theſe games; in France ſeldom, but in Switzerland, (where the greateſt liberty and familiarity is enjoyed amongſt the young people) they are numberleſs.——But the converſation hour is arrived, and our carriage is waiting.

Adieu.

## LETTER XXIV.

Palermo, June 28th.

THERE are two ſmall countries, one to the eaſt, the other to the weſt of this city, where the principal nobility have their country palaces. Both theſe we have viſited; there are many noble houſes in each of them. That to the eaſt is called La Bagaria, that to the weſt Il Colle.—We are this inſtant returned from La Bagaria, and I haſten to give you an account of the ridiculous things we have ſeen, though perhaps you will not thank me for it.

The palace of the Prince of Valguarnera is, I think, by much the fineſt and moſt beautiful of all the houſes of the Bagaria; but it is far from being the moſt extraordinary: were I to deſcribe it, I ſhould only tell you of things you have often ſeen and heard of in in other countries, ſo I ſhall only ſpeak of one, which, for its ſingularity, certainly is not to be paralleled on the face of the earth; it belongs to the prince of P——, a man of immenſe fortune, who has devoted his whole life to the ſtudy of monſters and chimeras, greater and more ridiculous than ever entered into the imagination of the wildeſt writers of romance or knight-errantry.

The amazing crowd of ſtatues that ſurround his houſe, appear at a diſtance like a little army drawn up for its defence; but when you get amongſt them, and every one aſſumes his true likeneſs, you imagine you have got into the regions of deluſion and enchantment; for of all that immenſe group, there is not one made to repreſent any object in nature; nor is the abſurdity of the wretched imagination that created them leſs aſtoniſhing than its wonderful fertility. It would require a volume

to

to deſcribe the whole, and a ſad volume indeed it would make. He has put the heads of men to the bodies of every ſort of animal, and the heads of every other animal to the bodies of men. Sometimes he makes a compound of five or ſix animals that have no ſort of reſemblance in nature. He puts the head of a lion to the neck of a gooſe, the body of a lizard, the legs of a goat, the tail of a fox. On the back of this monſter, he puts another, if poſſible ſtill more hideous, with five or ſix heads, and and a buſh of horns, that beats the beaſt in the Revelations all to nothing. There is no kind of horn in the world that he has not collected; and his pleaſure is, to ſee them all flouriſhing upon the ſame head. This is a ſtrange ſpecies of madneſs; and it is truly unaccountable that he has not been ſhut up many years ago; but he is perfectly innocent, and troubles nobody by the indulgence of his phrenzy; on the

contrary,

contrary, he gives bread to a number of statuaries and other workmen, whom he rewards in proportion as they can bring their imaginations to coincide with his own; or, in other words, according to the hideousness of the monsters they produce. It would be idle and tiresome to be particular in an account of these absurdities. The statues that adorn, or rather deform the great avenue, and surround the court of the palace, amount already to 600, notwithstanding which, it may be truly said, that he has not broke the second commandment; for of all that number, there is not the likeness of any thing in heaven above, in the earth beneath, or in the waters under the earth. The old ornaments which were put up by his father, who was a sensible man, appear to have been in a good taste. They have all been knocked to pieces, and laid together in a heap, to make room for this new creation.

The

The inside of this inchanted castle corresponds exactly with the out; it is in every respect as whimsical and fantastical, and you cannot turn yourself to any side, where you are not stared in the face by some hideous figure or other. Some of the apartments are spacious and magnificent, with high arched roofs; which instead of plaister or stucco, are composed entirely of large mirrors, nicely joined together. The effect that these produce (as each of them make a small angle with the other,) is exactly that of a multiplying glass; so that when three or four people are walking below, there is always the appearance of three or four hundred walking above. The whole of the doors are likewise covered over with small pieces of mirror, cut into the most ridiculous shapes, and intermixed with a great variety of chrystal and glass of different colours. All the chimney-pieces, windows, and side-boards are crouded with pyramids and pillars of tea-pots, caudle-cups, bowls, cups, ſaucers, &c. ſtrongly cemented together; ſome of theſe columns are not without their beauty: one of them has a large china chamber-pot for its baſe, and a circle of pretty little flower-pots for its capital: the ſhaft of the column, upwards of four feet long, is compoſed entirely of tea-pots of different ſizes, diminiſhing gradually from the baſe to the capital. The profuſion of china that has been employed in forming theſe columns is incredible; I dare ſay there is not leſs than forty pillars and pyramids formed in this ſtrange fantaſtic manner.

Moſt of the rooms are paved with fine marble tables of different colours, that look like ſo many tomb-ſtones. Some of theſe are richly wrought with lapis lazuli, porphyry, and other valuable ſtones; their fine poliſh is now gone, and they only appear like common marble; the place of theſe beautiful tables he has ſupplied by a new ſet of his own invention, ſome of which are not without their merit. Theſe are made of the fineſt tortoiſe-ſhell mixed with mother of pearl, ivory, and a variety of metals; and are mounted on fine ſtands of ſolid braſs.

The windows of this inchanted caſtle are compoſed of a variety of glaſs of every different colour, mixed without any ſort of order or regularity. Blue, red, green, yellow, purple, violet.—So that at each window, you may have the heavens and earth of whatever colour you chuſe, only by looking through the pane that pleaſes you.

The houſe clock is caſed in the body of a ſtatue; the eyes of the figure move with the pendulum, turning up their white and black alternately, and make a hideous appearance.

His bed-chamber and dreſſing-room are like two apartments in Noah's ark; there is ſcarce a beaſt, however vile, that he has not placed there; toads, frogs, ſerpents, lizards, ſcorpions, all cut out in marble, of their reſpective colours. There are a good many buſts too, that are not leſs ſingularly imagined.—Some of theſe make a very handſome profile on one ſide; turn to the other, and you have a ſkeleton; here you ſee a nurſe with a child in her arms; its back is exactly that of an infant; its face is that of a wrinkled old woman of ninety.

For ſome minutes one can laugh at theſe follies, but indignation and contempt ſoon get the better of your mirth, and the laugh is turned into a ſneer. I own I was ſoon tired of them; though ſome things are ſo ſtrangely fancied, that it may well excuſe a little mirth, even from the moſt rigid cynic.

The family statues are charming; they have been done from some old pictures, and make a most venerable appearance; he has dressed them out from head to foot, in new and elegant suits of marble; and indeed the effect it produces is more ridiculous than any thing you can conceive. Their shoes are all of black marble, their stockings generally of red; their cloaths are of different colours, blue, green, and variegated, with a rich lace of *giall' antique*. The perriwigs of the men and head-dresses of the ladies are of fine white; so are their shirts, with long flowing ruffles of alabaster. The walls of the house are covered with some fine basso relievos of white marble, in a good taste; these he could not well take out, or alter, so he has only added immense frames to them. Each frame is composed of four large marble tables.

The author and owner of this singular collection is a poor miserable lean figure, ſhivering at a breeze, and ſeems to be afraid of every body he ſpeaks to; but (what ſurpriſed me) I have heard him talk ſpeciouſly enough on ſeveral occaſions. He is one of the richeſt ſubjects in the iſland, and it is thought he has not laid out leſs than 20,000 pounds in the creation of this world of monſters and chimeras.—He certainly might have fallen upon ſome way to prove himſelf a fool at a cheaper rate. However it gives bread to a number of poor people, to whom he is an excellent maſter. His houſe at Palermo is a good deal in the ſame ſtile: his carriages are covered with plates of braſs, ſo that I really believe ſome of them are muſket proof.

The government have had ſerious thoughts of demoliſhing the regiment of monſters he has placed round his houſe, but as he is humane and inoffenſive, and as this would certainly break his heart, they have as yet forborne. However, the ſeeing of them

by

by women with child is ſaid to have been already attended with very unfortunate circumſtances; ſeveral living monſters having been brought forth in the neighbourhood. The ladies complain that they dare no longer take an airing in the Bagaria; that ſome hideous form always haunts their imagination for ſome time after: their huſbands too, it is ſaid, are as little ſatisfied with the great variety of horns. Adieu. I ſhall write you again by next poſt, as matter multiplies faſt upon me in this metropolis.

Ever your's.

## LETTER XXV.

Palermo, June 30th.

THE account the people here give of the Sirocc, or South-eaſt wind, is truly wonderful; to-day, at the viceroy's, we were complaining of the violence of the heat, the thermometer being at 79.— They aſſured us, that if we ſtaid till the end of next month, we ſhould probably look on this as pleaſant cool weather; adding, that if we had once experienced the Sirocc, all other weather will appear temperate.—I aſked to what degree the thermometer commonly roſe during this wind; but found to my ſurprize, that there was no ſuch inſtrument in uſe amongſt them: however, the violence of it, they aſſure us, is incredible; and that thoſe who had remained many years in Spain and

and Malta, had never felt any heat in thoſe countries to compare to it.—How it happens to be more violent in Palermo than in any other part of Sicily, is a myſtery that ſtill remains to be unfolded. Several treatiſes have been written on this ſubject, but none that give any tolerable degree of ſatisfaction. As we ſhall ſtay for ſome time longer, it is poſſible we may have an opportunity of giving you ſome account of it.

They have begun ſome weeks ago to make preparations for the great feaſt of St. Roſolia; and our friends here ſay they are determined that we ſhall not leave them till after it is over; but this I am afraid will not be in our power. The warm ſeaſon advances, and the time we appointed for our return to Naples is already elapſed; but indeed, return when we will, we ſhall make but a bad exchange; and were it not for thoſe of our own country whom we have left behind us, we certainly ſhould have determined on a much longer ſtay. But although the ſociety here is ſuperior to that of Naples, yet,—call it prejudice—or call it what you will, there is a—*je ne ſçai quoi*,—a certain confidence in the character, the worth, and friendſhip of our own people, that I have ſeldom felt any where on the continent, except in Switzerland. This ſenſation, which conſtitutes the charm of ſociety, and can alone render it ſupportable for any time, is only inſpired by ſomething analogous, and ſympathetic, in our feelings and ſentiments; like two inſtruments that are in uniſon, and vibrate to each other's touch: for ſociety is a concert, and if the inſtruments are not in tune, there never can be harmony; and (to carry on the metaphor) this harmony too muſt ſometimes be heightened and ſupported by the introduction of a diſcord; but where diſcords predominate,

which

which is often the caſe between an Engliſh and an Italian mind, the muſick muſt be wretched indeed.—Had we but a little mixture of our own ſociety, how gladly ſhould we ſpend the winter in Sicily; but we often think with regret on Mr. Hamilton's and Mr. Walter's families; and wiſh again to be on the continent.—Indeed, even the pleaſures we enjoy here, we owe principally to Mr. Hamilton: his recommendations we have ever found to be the beſt paſſport and introduction; and the zeal and cordiality with which theſe are always received, proceeds evidently not from motives of deference and reſpect to the miniſter, but of love and affection to the man.

This morning we went to ſee a celebrated convent of Capuchins, about a mile without the city; it contains nothing very remarkable but the burial place, which indeed is a great curioſity. This is a

vaſt

vaſt ſubterraneous apartment, divided into large commodious galleries, the walls on each ſide of which are hollowed into a variety of niches, as if intended for a great collection of ſtatues; theſe niches, inſtead of ſtatues, are all filled with dead bodies, ſet upright upon their legs, and fixed by the back to the inſide of the nich: their number is about three hundred: they are all dreſſed in the clothes they uſually wore, and form a moſt reſpectable and venerable aſſembly. The ſkin and muſcles, by a certain preparation, become as dry and hard as a piece of ſtock-fiſh; and although many of them have been here upwards of two hundred and fifty years, yet none are reduced to ſkeletons; the muſcles, indeed, in ſome appear to be a good deal more ſhrunk than in others; probably becauſe theſe perſons had been more extenuated at the time of their death.

Here

Here the people of Palermo pay daily visits to their deceased friends, and recal with pleasure and regret the scenes of their past life: here they familiarize themselves with their future state, and chuse the company they would wish to keep in the other world. It is a common thing to make choice of their nich, and to try if their body fits it, that no alterations may be necessary after they are dead; and sometimes, by way of a voluntary penance, they accustom themselves to stand for hours in these niches.

The bodies of the princes and first nobility are lodged in handsome chests or trunks, some of them richly adorned: these are not in the shape of coffins, but all of one width, and about a foot and a half, or two feet deep. The keys are kept by the nearest relations of the family, who

who ſometimes come and drop a tear over their departed friends.

I am not ſure if this is not a better method of diſpoſing of the dead than ours. Theſe viſits muſt prove admirable leſſons of humility; and I aſſure you, they are not ſuch objects of horror as you would imagine: they are ſaid, even for ages after death, to retain a ſtrong likeneſs to what they were when alive; ſo that, as ſoon as you have conquered the firſt feelings excited by theſe venerable figures, you only conſider this as a vaſt gallery of original portraits, drawn after the life, by the juſteſt and moſt unprejudiced hand. It muſt be owned that the colours are rather faded; and the pencil does not appear to have been the moſt flattering in the world; but no matter, it is the pencil of truth, and not of a mercenary, who only wants to pleaſe.

We

We were alleging too, that it might be made of very conſiderable utility to ſociety; and that theſe dumb orators could give the moſt pathetic lectures upon pride and vanity. Whenever a fellow began to ſtrut, like Mr. B. or to affect the haughty ſupercilious air, he ſhould be ſent to converſe with his friends in the gallery; and if their arguments did not bring him to a proper way of thinking, I would give him up as incorrigible.

At Bologna they ſhewed us the ſkeleton of a celebrated beauty, who died at a period of life when ſhe was ſtill the object of univerſal admiration. By way of making atonement for her own vanity, ſhe bequeathed herſelf as a monument, to curb the vanity of others. Recollecting on her death-bed the great adulation that had been paid to her charms, and the fatal change they were ſoon to undergo, ſhe ordered

ordered that her body ſhould be diſſected, and her bones hung up for the inſpection of all young maidens who are inclined to be vain of their beauty. However, if ſhe had been preſerved in this moral gallery, the leſſon would have been ſtronger; for thoſe very features that had raiſed her vanity would ſtill have remained, only diveſted of all their power, and diſarmed of every charm.

Some of the Capuchins ſleep in theſe galleries every night, and pretend to have many wonderful viſions and revelations; but the truth is, that very few people believe them.

No woman is ever admitted into this convent either dead or alive; and this interdiction is written in large characters over the gate. The poor indolent Capuchins, the fraileſt of all fleſh, have great need

need of such precautions: they have no occupation from without, and they have no resources within themselves, so that they must be an easy prey to every temptation:—Bocaccio, and all the books of that kind, are filled with stories of their frailty.—Yesterday, dining at the Prince of Sperlinga's, and talking on this subject, the Abbé T—— gave us an anecdote of a friend of his, who was formerly a brother of this convent. He is known by the name of Fra Pasqual, and has passed through many singular scenes of life, which it would be too long to recount. His last migration, or, if you will, transmigration, was from one of the banditti of this kingdom, in which capacity he had been enrolled for some time; but, tired of the danger and fatigue to which he was perpetually exposed, he at last determined to exchange the character of the hero, for that of the saint, and try if it was not both ſafer and ſurer, to rely on the weakneſs of others, than on our own ſtrength.

Fra Paſqual pretended a ſtrong compunction for the tranſgreſſions of his paſt life, and made a promiſe to the Virgin, that the remainder of it ſhould be ſpent in mortification and penance, to atone for them. To this end, Paſqual took the vows of poverty and of chaſtity, and entered into all the rigours of the monaſtic life.—For ſome weeks he behaved in a moſt exemplary manner; he went barefooted, wore a large roſary, and a thicker cord of diſcipline than any monk in the convent; and his whole deportment gave teſtimony of the moſt unfeigned repentance; however, the devil was ſtill at work in the heart of Paſqual, and all theſe external mortifications only made him work the harder; in ſhort, he found it impoſſible to drive him out: Paſqual was ſenſible of

this;

this; and afraid lest the enemy should at last get the better of him, he thought it advisable to leave at Palermo the character of sanctity he had acquired, and begin somewhere else upon a new score. He embarked for Naples, where he was soon admitted into a Capuchin convent.

As Pasqual knew from experience that the dull uniformity of the monastic life required some little amusements to render it supportable, the first thing he set about was to find a mistress. He made love to a lady of easy virtue, who soon admitted his addresses, but at the same time informed him, that he had a formidable rival, who was jealous as a tiger, and would not fail to put them both to death, should he discover the intrigue. This was no other than a lifeguard-man, a fellow of six feet two inches, with a vast spada, like that of Goliah, and a monstrous pair of curled whiskers, that would have caſt a damp on the heart of any man but Fra Paſqual; but the monaſtic life had not yet enervated him; he was accuſtomed to danger, and loved a few difficulties: however, as in his preſent character he could not be on a footing with his rival, he thought it beſt only to make uſe of prudence and ſtratagem to ſupplant him: theſe are the eccleſiaſtical arms, and they have generally been found too hard for the military.

The lady promiſed him an interview as ſoon as the court ſhould go to Portici, where the lifeguard-man's duty obliged him to attend the king. Paſqual waited with impatience for ſome time; at laſt the wiſhed-for night arrived; the king ſet off, after the opera, with all his guards. Paſqual flew like lightning to the arms of his miſtreſs; the preliminaries were ſoon ſettled, and the happy lovers had juſt fallen aſleep, when they were ſuddenly alarmed

alarmed by a rap and a well known voice at the door. The lady ſtarted up in an agony of deſpair, aſſuring Paſqual that they were both undone; that this was her lover; and if ſome expedient was not fallen upon, in the firſt tranſports of his fury, he would certainly put them both to death. There was no time for reflection; the lifeguard-man demanded entrance in the moſt peremptory manner, and the lady was obliged to inſtant compliance. Paſqual had juſt time to gather his rags together, and cram himſelf in below the bed; at that inſtant the door opened, and the giant came in, rattling his arms and ſtorming at his miſtreſs, for having made him wait ſo long; however, ſhe ſoon pacified him. He then ordered her to ſtrike a light, that he might ſee to undreſs: —this ſtruck Paſqual to the ſoul, and he gave himſelf up for loſt; however, the lady's addreſs ſaved him, when he leaſt expected it. In bringing the tinder, ſhe took care to let fall ſome water into the box; and all the beating ſhe and her lover could beat, they could not produce one ſpark. Every ſtroke of the flint ſounded in Paſqual's ears like his death-knell; but when he heard the lifeguard-man ſwearing at the tinder for not kindling, he began to conceive ſome hopes, and bleſſed the fertile invention of woman.—The lady told him he might eaſily get a light at the guard, which was at no great diſtance. —Paſqual's heart leaped with joy;— but when the ſoldier anſwered that he was abſent without leave, and durſt not be ſeen, it again began to flag; but on his ordering *her* to go—it died within him, and he now found himſelf in greater danger than ever. The lady herſelf was diſconcerted; but quickly recovering, ſhe told him, it would be too long before ſhe could get dreſſed; but adviſed him to go to the corner of a neighbouring ſtreet, where there was a lamp burning before

the

the Virgin Mary, who could have no objection to his lighting a candle at it.—Pasqual revived;—but the soldier declared he was too much fatigued with his walk, and would rather undress in the dark; he at the same time began to grope below the bed for a bottle of liqueurs, which he knew stood there.—Pasqual shook like a quaker,—however, still he escaped.—The lady observing what he was about, made a spring, and got him the bottle, at the very instant he was within an inch of seizing Pasqual's head.—The lady then went to bed, and told her lover, as it was a cold night, she would warm his place for him. Pasqual admired her address, and began to conceive some hopes of escaping.

His situation was the most irksome in the world; the bed was so low, that he had no room to move; and when the great heavy lifeguard-man entered it, he found himself squeezed down to the ground: He lay trembling and stifling his breath for some time, but found it absolutely impossible to support his situation till morning; and indeed, if it had, his clothes, which were scattered about, must infallibly discover him: he therefore began to think of making his escape; but he could not move without alarming his rival, who was now lying above him. At first he thought of rushing suddenly out, and throwing himself into the street; but this he disdained, and, on second thoughts, determined to seize the lifeguard-man's sword, and either put him to death, or make an honourable capitulation both for himself and the lady. In the midst of these reflections, his rival began to snore, and Pasqual declares that no musick was ever so grateful to his soul. He tried to stir a little, and finding that it did not awake the enemy, he by degrees worked himself out of his prison. He immediately laid

hold

hold of the great spada;—when all his fears forsook him, and he felt as bold as a lion. He now relinquished the dastardly scheme of escaping, and only thought how he could best retaliate on his rival, for all that he had made him suffer.

As Pasqual was stark naked, it was no more trouble to him to put on the soldier's clothes than his own; and as both his cloak and his cappouch together were not worth a sixpence, he thought it most eligible to equip himself à la militaire, and to leave his sacerdotal robes to the soldier. In a short time he was dressed cap-a-pie. His greasy cowl, his cloak, his sandals, his rosary, and his rope of discipline, he gathered together, and placed on a chair before the bed; and girding himself with a great buff belt, instead of the cordon of St. Francis, and grasping his trusty Toledo instead of the crucifix, he sallied forth into the street. He pondered for

some

ſome time what ſcheme to fall upon; and at firſt thought of returning in the character of another lifeguard-man, pretending to have been ſent by the officer with a guard in queſt of his companion, who not being found in his quarters, was ſuppoſed to have deſerted: and thus, after having made him pay heartily for all that he had ſuffered under the bed, to leave him to the enjoyment of his pannic, and the elegant ſuit of clothes he had provided him. However, he was not ſatisfied with this revenge, and determined on one ſtill more ſolid. He went to the guard, and told the officer that he had met a Capuchin friar, with all the enſigns of his ſanctity about him, ſculking through the ſtreets, in the dead of night, when they pretend to be employed in prayer for the ſins of mankind. That prompted by curioſity to follow him, the holy friar as he expected went ſtraight to the houſe of a celebrated courtezan; that he ſaw him admitted,

admitted, and listened at the window till he heard them go to bed together: that if he did not find this information to be true, he should resign himself his prisoner, and submit to whatever punishment he should think proper.

The officer and his guard delighted to have such a hold of a Capuchin, (who pretend to be the very models of sanctity, and who revile in a particular manner the licentious life of the military) turned out with the utmost alacrity, and, under the conduct of Pasqual, surrounded the lady's house. Pasqual began thundering at the door; and demanded entrance for the officer and his guard. The unhappy soldier waking with the noise, and not doubting that it was a detachment sent to seize him, gave himself up to despair, and instantly took shelter in the very place that Pasqual had so lately occupied; at the same time laying hold of all the things he

found

found on the chair; never doubting that they were his own clothes. As the lady was somewhat dilatory in opening the door, Pasqual pretended to put his foot to it, when up it flew, and entering with the officer and his guard, demanded the body of a Capuchin friar, who they were informed, lodged with her that night. The lady had heard Pasqual go out, and having no suspicion that he would inform against himself, she protested her innocence in the most solemn manner, taking all the saints to witness that she knew no such person: but Pasqual suspecting the retreat of the lover, began groping below the bed, and soon pulled out his own greasy cowl and cloak;—"Here (said he to the officer)—"here are proofs enough:—I'll answer for "it, *Signor Padre* himself is at no great "distance."—And putting his nose below the bed;—"Fogh (says he) I smell him;—"he stinks like a fox. The surest method "of finding a Capuchin, is by the nose; "you

"you may wind him a mile off."—Then lowering their lanthorn, they beheld the unfortunate lover ſqueezed in betwixt the bed and the ground, and almoſt ſtifled.— "*Ecco lo*, (ſaid Paſqual) here he is, with "all the enſigns of his holineſs;" and pulling them out one by one,—the crucifix, the roſary, and the cord of diſcipline.— "You may ſee (ſaid he) that the reverend "father came here to do penance;"—and taking up the cord,—"Suppoſe now we "ſhould aſſiſt him in this meritorious "work. *Andiamo, Signor Padre,—andiamo.*—We will ſave you the trouble of "inflicting it yourſelf;—and whether you "came here to ſin, or to repent, by your "own maxims, you know, a little ſound "diſcipline is healthful to the ſoul."—The guard were lying round the bed, in convulſions of laughter; and began breaking the moſt galling and moſt inſolent jokes upon the ſuppoſed padre.—The lifeguard-man thought himſelf enchanted.—He at laſt ventured to ſpeak, and declared they were all in a miſtake;—that he was no Capuchin:—upon which the laugh redoubled, and the coarſeſt jokes were repeated. The lady, in the mean time, with the beſt diſſembled marks of fear and aſtoniſhment, ran about the room, exclaiming—"*Oime Siamo Perduti,—Siamo* "*incantati,—Siamo inſorcelati.*"—Paſqual delighted to ſee that his plan had taken its full effect, thought it now time to make his retreat, before the unfortunate lover could have an opportunity of examining his clothes; and perhaps detecting him: he therefore pretended regimental buſineſs, and regretting much that he was obliged to join his corps; took leave of the officer and his guard; at the ſame time recommending by all means, to treat the holy father with all that reverence and reſpect that was due to ſo ſacred a perſon.

The

The lifeguard-man, when he got out from below the bed, began to look about for his clothes; but obſerving nothing but the greaſy weeds of a Capuchin friar, he was now perfectly convinced, that Heaven had delivered him over, for his offences, to the power of ſome dæmon; (for of all mortals, the Neapolitan ſoldiers are the moſt ſuperſtitious)—The lady too, acted her part ſo well, that he had no longer any doubt of it.—" Thus it is (ſaid he in a " penitential voice) to offend heaven!—I " own my ſin.—I knew it was Friday, and " yet—O, fleſh, fleſh!—Had it been any " other day, I ſtill ſhould have remained " what I was.—O, St. Gennaro! I paſs'd " thee * too without paying the due " reſpect:—thy all-ſeeing eye has found " me out. Gentlemen, do with me what " you pleaſe;—I am not what I ſeem to

* A celebrated ſtatue of St. Januarius, betwixt Portici and Naples.

"be."—"No, no (ſaid the officer) we "are ſenſible of that.—But, come, Signor "Padre, on with your garments, and "march;—we have no time to trifle.— "Here, Corporal—(giving him the cordon) "tie his hands, and let him feel the weight "of St. Francis.—The ſaint owes him that, "for having ſo impudently denied him for "his maſter."—The poor ſoldier was perfectly paſſive;—they arrayed him in the ſandals, the cowl, and the cloak of Fra Paſqual, and put the great roſary about his neck; and a moſt woeful figure he made.—The officer made him look in the glaſs, to try if he could recollect himſelf, and aſked if he was a Capuchin now or not.—He was ſhocked at his own appearance; but bore every thing with meekneſs and reſignation. They then conducted him to the guard, belabouring him all the way with the cord of St. Francis, and aſking him every ſtroke, if he knew his maſter now?—

In

In the mean time, Paſqual was ſnug in his convent, enjoying the ſweets of his adventure. He had a ſpare cloak and cowl, and was ſoon equipped again like one of the holy fathers; he then took the clothes and accoutrements of the lifeguard-man, and laid them in a heap, near the gate of another convent of Capuchins, but at a great diſtance from his own, reſerving only to himſelf a trifle of money which he found in the breeches pocket, juſt to indemnify him for the loſs of his cloak and his cowl; and even this, he ſays, he ſhould have held ſacred, but he knew whoever ſhould find the clothes, would make lawful prize of it.

The poor ſoldier remained next day a ſpectacle of ridicule to all the world; at laſt his companions heard of his ſtrange metamorphoſis, and came in troops to ſee him: their jokes were perhaps ſtill more galling than thoſe of the guard, but as he

 thought

thought himſelf under the finger of God, or at leaſt of St. Januarius, he bore all with meekneſs and patience; at laſt his clothes were found, and he was ſet at liberty; but he believes to this day, that the whole was the work of the devil, ſent to chaſtize him for his ſins; and has never ſince ſeen his miſtreſs on a Friday, nor paſſed the ſtatue of St. Januarius without muttering a prayer. Fra Paſqual has told the ſtory to ſeveral of his moſt intimate friends, whom he can depend on, amongſt whom is the Abbé T-t-i, who has often had it from his own mouth.

I beg pardon for this long ſtory; had I ſuſpected that it would have run out to half this length, I aſſure you, I ſhould not have troubled you with it. Perhaps, however, you will think this apology preciſely the moſt unneceſſary, and moſt impertinent part of it all.—This is often the fate of apologies, particularly for long letters; First, because it always makes them longer;—Secondly,—Hey-day! where are we going now?—To return then to our subject. We had no sooner left the Capuchin convent, than our carriage broke down, long before we reached the city: and as walking (at Palermo as well as Naples) is of all things the most disgraceful, we risked by this unfortunate accident to have our characters blasted for ever. However, Philip, our Sicilian servant, took care to make such a noise about it, that our dignity did not much suffer. He kept a little distance before us, pesting and blasting all the way at their cursed crazy carriages;—and swearing that there never was any thing in the world so infamous: that in a city like Palermo, the capital of all Sicily, Signori of our rank and dignity should be obliged to walk on foot; that it must be an eternal reflection against the place;—and bawled out to every person he met, if there was no coaches to be had; no carriages of any kind, either for love or money. In ſhort, we had not got half through the ſtreet, before we had ſeveral offers from gentlemen of our acquaintance, who lamented exceedingly the indignity we had ſuffered, and wondered much, that we did not rather ſend forward a ſervant for another coach, and wait (in the heat of the ſun) till it arrived.

This is not the only time that Philip's wits have been of ſervice to us on ſuch occaſions. A few nights ago, we had a diſpute with our coachman; turned him off, and had not provided another. We were unfortunately engaged to go to the great converſation. What was to be done?—No ſuch thing as walking.—Should we be caught in the fact, we are diſgraced for ever.—It would be worſe than to be caught in that of adultery.—No alternative, however. There was not a coach to be had, and our old coachman would not ſerve us for one night only.—Philip made ſad wry faces, and ſwore the coachman ought to be crucified;—but when he ſaw us bent on walking, he was ſtill more diſtreſſed; and I really believe, if we had been diſcovered, that he would not have ſerved us any longer. He therefore ſet his wits to work, how he ſhould preſerve both his maſters' honour and his own place. He at firſt heſitated, before he would take up the flambeau; but he would by no means be prevailed on to light it.—"What, "(ſaid Philip) do you think I have no "more regard for you, than to expoſe you "to the eyes of the whole world? No, no, "Gentlemen; if you will bring yourſelves "to diſgrace, you ſhall not at leaſt make "me the agent of ſhewing it: but remem- "ber, if you are obſerved walking, no "mortal will believe you keep a coach; "and do you expect after that to be re- "ceived into company?"—"Well, well,

" Philip, do as you please, but we must go " to the conversation."—Philip shrugged up his shoulders.—" *Diabolo—che faremo!* " *Andiamo dunque Signori—andiamo.*"— So saying, he led the way, and we followed.

Philip had studied the geography of the town; he conducted us through lanes only known to himself, and carefully avoided the great street; till at last we arrived at a little entry, which leads to the conversation rooms; here the carriages usually stop. We slipped up the entry in the dark; when Philip, darting into a shop, lighted his flambeau in an instant, and came rushing before us, bawling out,—" *Piazza per gli* " *Signori forrestieri;*"—when all the world immediately made way for us.—After we had got into the rooms, he called so loud after us, asking at what time he should order the coach to return; that, overcome partly by risibility, and partly by a consciousness

ſciouſneſs of the deceit, not one of us had power to anſwer him. Philip, however, followed us, and repeated the queſtion ſo often, that we were obliged to give him a reply, "*a mezzo notte.*"—At midnight he came to tell us that the coach was ready.—We were curious to ſee how he would behave on this occaſion; for it was not half ſo difficult to get in unobſerved, as to get out: however, Philip's genius was equal to both.—So ſoon as we got into the entry, he run to the door, bawling out Antonio, as hard as he could roar.—No Antonio anſwered;—and unfortunately, there was a number of gentlemen and ladies going away at the ſame time. They begged of us, as ſtrangers, to ſtep firſt into our carriage, and abſolutely refuſed to go out before us.—Philip was ſadly puzzled.—He firſt ran up the ſtreet, then he ran down, and came back all out of breath, curſing Antonio. "That raſcal (ſaid he) is never "in the way, and you muſt turn him off.—

"He pretends that he could not get up his "coach to the door, for the great croud of "carriages; and is waiting about fifty "yards below.—Vostri Eccellenzi had better "step down (said Philip) otherwise you "will be obliged to wait here at least half "an hour."—We took leave of the company, and set off.—Philip ran like a lamp-lighter, till he had almost passed the carriages, when dashing his flambeau on the ground, as if by accident, he extinguished it, and getting into a narrow lane, he waited till we came up; when he whispered us to follow him,—and conducted us back, by the same labyrinth we had come; and thus saved us from eternal infamy.—However, he assures us, that he will not venture it again for his place.

Now, what do you think of a nation where such prejudices as these prevail?—It is pretty much the case all over Italy.—An Italian nobleman is ashamed of nothing so much

much as making uſe of his legs.—They think their dignity augments by the repoſe of their members; and that no man can be truly reſpectable, that does not loll away one half of his time on a ſofa, or in a carriage.—In ſhort, a man is obliged to be indolent and effeminate, not to be deſpiſed and ridiculous.—What can we expect of ſuch a people?—Can they be capable of any thing great or manly, who ſeem almoſt aſhamed to appear men!—I own, it ſurpaſſes my comprehenſion; and I bleſs my ſtars every time that I think of honeſt John Bull, even with all his faults.—Will you believe me, that, of all that I have known in Italy, there are ſcarce half a dozen that have had fortitude enough to ſubdue this moſt contemptible of all human prejudices?—The Prince of Campo Franco too in this place, is above it. He is a noble fellow, and both in his perſon and character, greatly reſembles our late worthy friend, General Craufurd. He is a major-general too, and always dresses in his uniform, which still increases the resemblance. Every time I see him, he says or does something that recalls strongly to my mind the idea of our noble general.—He laughs at the follies of his country, and holds these wretched prejudices in that contempt they deserve.— "What would the old hardy Romans think "(said he, talking on this subject) were "they permitted to take a view of the occupations of their progeny?—I should "like to see a Brutus or a Cassius amongst "us for a little;—how the clumsy vulgar "fellows would be hooted.—I dare say "they would soon be glad to return to the "shades again."

Adieu;—for fome nights past we have been observing the course of a comet; and as we were the first people here that took notice of it, I assure you, we are looked upon as very profound astronomers. I shall say more of it next letter.—We have now

got

got out of our abominable inn, and have taken a final leave of our French landlady. The Count Bushemi, a very amiable young man, has been kind enough to provide us a lodging on the sea-shore; one of the coolest and most agreeable in Palermo.

Ever yours, &c.

## LETTER XXVI.

Palermo, July 2d.

OUR comet is now gone; we first observed it on the 24th. It had no tail, but was surrounded with a faintish ill defined light, that made it look like a bright star shining through a thin cloud. This, in all probability, is owing to an atmosphere, around the body of the comet, that causes a refraction of the rays, and prevents them from reaching us with that distinctness we observe in bodies that have no atmosphere. —We were still the more persuaded of this two nights ago, when we had the good fortune to catch the comet just passing close by a small fixed star, whose light was not only considerably dimm'd, but we thought we observed a sensible change of place in the star, as soon as its rays fell into the atmo-

atmosphere of the comet; owing no doubt to the refraction in passing through that atmosphere.—We attempted to trace the line of the comet's course, but as we could find no globe, it was not possible to do it with any degree of precision.—Its direction was almost due north, and its velocity altogether amazing.—We did not observe it so minutely the two or three first nights of its appearance, but on the 30th it was at our zenith here, (latitude 38° 10′; longitude from Lond. 13°) about five minutes after midnight, and last night, the first of July, it passed four degrees to the east of the polar star, nearly at 40 minutes after eight. So that, in less than 24 hours, it has described a great arch in the heavens, upwards of 50 degrees; which gives an idea of the most amazing velocity. Supposing it at the distance of the sun, at this rate of travelling, it would go round the earth's orbit in less than a week. Which makes, I think, considerably more than sixty millions

lions of miles in a day; a motion that vastly surpasses all human comprehension. And as this motion continues to be greatly accelerated, what must it be, when the comet approaches still nearer to the body of the sun! Last night a change of place was observable in the space of a few minutes, particularly when it passed near any of the fixed stars. We attempted to find if it had any observable parallax, but the vast rapidity of its motion always prevented us; for whatever fixed stars it was near in the horizon, it had got so far to the north of them, long before it reached the meridian, that the parallax, if there was any, entirely escaped us.

I shall long much to see the observations that have been made with you, and in other distant countries, on this comet; as from these, we shall probably be enabled to form some judgment of its distance from the earth; which, although we could observe

no

no parallax, I am apt to believe was not very great, as its motion was ſo very perceptible.—We could procure no inſtruments to meaſure its apparent diſtance from any of the fixed ſtars, ſo that the only two obſervations any thing can be made of, are, the time of its paſſing the polar ſtar laſt night, its diſtance from it, and the time of its arrival at our zenith on the 30th; this we found by applying the eye to a ſtraight rod, hung perpendicularly from a ſmall thread. The comet was not in the exact point of the zenith, but to the beſt of our obſervation, about ſix or ſeven minutes to the north of it. Laſt night it was viſible almoſt immediately after ſun-ſet; long before any of the fixed ſtars appeared. It is now immerſed in the rays of the ſun, and has certainly got very near his body. If it returns again to the regions of ſpace, it will probably be viſible in a few days, but I own I ſhould much doubt of any ſuch return, if it is really by the attractive force

of

of the ſun, that it is at preſent carried with ſuch amazing celerity towards him. This is the third comet of this kind, whoſe return I have had an opportunity of watching; but never was fortunate enough to find any of them after they had paſſed the ſun; though thoſe that do really return, appear at that time much more luminous than before they approached him.

The aſtronomy of comets, from what I can remember of it, appears to be clogged with very great difficulties, and even ſome ſeeming abſurdities. It is difficult to conceive, that theſe immenſe bodies, after being drawn to the ſun with the velocity of a million of miles in an hour; when they have at laſt come almoſt to touch him, ſhould then fly off from his body, with the ſame velocity they approached it; and that too, by the power of this very motion that his attraction has occaſioned.—The demonſtration of this I remember is very

curious

curious and ingenious; but I wish it may be entirely free from sophistry. No doubt, in bodies moving in curves round a fixed center, as the centripetal motion increases, the centrifugal one increases likewise;—but how this motion, which is only generated by the former, should at last get the better of the power that produces it; and that too, at the very time this power has acquired its utmost force and energy; seems somewhat difficult to conceive. It is the only instance I know, wherein the effect increasing regularly with the cause; at last, whilst the cause is still acting with full vigour; the effect entirely gets the better of the cause, and leaves it in the lurch. For, the body attracted, is at last carried away with infinite velocity from the attracting body.—By what power is it carried away?—Why, say our philosophers, by the very power of this attraction, which has now produced a new power superior to itself, to wit, the centrifugal force. However,

ever, perhaps all this may be reconcilable to reaſon; far be it from me to preſume attacking ſo glorious a ſyſtem as that of attraction. The law that the heavenly bodies are ſaid to obſerve, in deſcribing equal areas in equal times, is ſuppoſed to be demonſtrated, and by this it would appear, that the centripetal and centrifugal forces alternately get the maſtery of one another.

However, I cannot help thinking it ſomewhat hard to conceive, that gravity ſhould always get the better of the centrifugal force, at the very time that its action is the ſmalleſt, when the comet is at its greateſt diſtance from the ſun; and that the centrifugal force ſhould get the better of gravity, at the very time that its action is the greateſt, when the comet is at its neareſt point to the ſun.

To a common obſerver it would rather appear, that the ſun, like an electric body, after it had once charged the objects that it attracted with its own effluvia or atmosphere, by degrees loses its attraction, and at last even repels them; and, that the attracting power, like what we likewise observe in electricity, does not return again till the effluvia imbibed from the attracting body is dispelled or dissipated; when it is again attracted, and so on alternately. For it appears (at least to an unphilosophical observer) somewhat repugnant to reason, to say that a body flying off from another body some thousands of miles in a minute, should all the time be violently attracted by that body, and that it is even by virtue of this very attraction that it is flying off from it.—He would probably ask, What more could it do, pray, were it really to be repelled?

Had the system of electricity, and of repulsion as well as attraction, been known and established in the last age, I have little doubt that the profound genius of Newton would have called it to his aid; and perhaps accounted in a more ſatisfactory manner, for many of the great phænomena of the heavens. To the beſt of my remembrance, we know of no body that poſſeſſes, in any conſiderable degree, the power of attraction, that in certain circumſtances does not likewiſe poſſeſs the power of repulſion.—The magnet, the tourmalin, amber, glaſs, and every electrical ſubſtance. —Now from analogy, as we find the ſun ſo powerfully endowed with attraction, why may we not likewiſe ſuppoſe him to be poſſeſſed of repulſion? Indeed, this very power ſeems to be confeſſed by the Newtonians to reſide in the ſun in a moſt wonderful degree; for they aſſure us he repels the rays of light with ſuch amazing force, that they fly upwards of 80 millions of miles in ſeven minutes. Now why ſhould we confine this repulſion to the rays of light only?—As they are material, may not

other

other matter brought near his body, be affected in the ſame manner? Indeed one would imagine, that their motion alone would create the moſt violent repulſion; and that the force, with which they are perpetually flowing from the ſun, would moſt effectually prevent every other body from approaching him; for this we find is the conſtant effect of a rapid ſtream of any other matter.—But let us examine a little more his effects on comets. The tails of theſe bodies, are probably their atmoſpheres rendered highly electrical, either from the violence of their motion, or from their proximity to the ſun.—Of all the bodies we know, there is none in ſo conſtant and ſo violent an electrical ſtate, as the higher regions of our own atmoſphere. Of this I have long been convinced; for, ſend up a kite with a ſmall wire about its ſtring, only to the height of 12 or 1300 feet, and at all times it will produce fire, as I have found by frequent experience; ſometimes,

 when

when the air was perfectly clear, without a cloud in the hemiſphere; at other times, when it was thick and hazy, and totally unfit for electrical operations below. Now, as this is the caſe at ſo ſmall a height, and as we find the effect ſtill grows ſtronger, in proportion as the kite advances, (for I have ſometimes obſerved, that a little blaſt of wind, ſuddenly raiſing the kite about a hundred feet, has more than doubled the effect) what muſt it be in very great elevations?—Indeed we may often judge of it from the violence with which the clouds are agitated, from the meteors formed above the region of the clouds, and particularly from the aurora borealis, which has been obſerved to have much the ſame colour and appearance as the matter that forms the tails of comets.

Now what muſt be the effect of ſo vaſt a body as our atmoſphere, made ſtrongly electrical, when it happens to approach any

other

other body ?—It muſt always be either violently attracted or repelled, according to the poſitive or negative quality (in the language of electricians) of the body that it approaches.

It has ever been obſerved that the tails of comets (juſt as we ſhould expect, from a very light fluid body, attached to a ſolid heavy one) are drawn after the comets, as long as they are at a diſtance from the ſun; but ſo ſoon as the comet gets near his body, the tail veers about to that ſide of the comet that is in the oppoſite direction from the ſun, and no longer follows the comet, but continues its motion ſideways, oppoſing its whole length to the medium through which it paſſes, rather than allow it in any degree to approach the ſun. Indeed, its tendency to follow the body of the comet is ſtill obſervable, were it not prevented by ſome force ſuperior to that tendency; for the tail is always obſerved to bend a little to that ſide from whence the comet is flying. This perhaps is ſome proof too, that it does not move in an abſolute vacuum.

When the comet reaches its perihelion, the tail is generally very much lengthened, perhaps by the rarefaction from the heat; —perhaps by the increaſe of the ſun's repulſion, or that of his atmoſphere. It ſtill continues projected, exactly in the oppoſite direction from the ſun; and when the comet moves off again to the regions of ſpace, the tail, inſtead of following it, as it did on its approach, is projected a vaſt way before it, and ſtill keeps the body of the comet exactly oppoſed betwixt it and the ſun; till by degrees, as the diſtance increaſes, the length of the tail is diminiſhed; the repulſion probably becoming weaker and weaker.

It has likewiſe been obſerved, that the length of theſe tails are commonly in proportion to the proximity of the comet to the ſun. That of 1680 threw out a train that would almoſt have reached from the ſun to the earth. If this had been attracted by the ſun, would it not have fallen upon his body? when the comet at that time was not one fourth of his diameter diſtant from him; but inſtead of this, it was darted away to the oppoſite ſide of the heavens, even with a greater velocity than that of the comet itſelf—Now what can this be owing to, if not to a repulſive power in the ſun, or his atmoſphere?

And, indeed, it would at firſt appear but little leſs abſurd to ſay, that the tail of the comet is all this time violently attracted by the ſun, although it be driven away in an oppoſite direction from him, as to ſay the ſame of the comet itſelf. It is true, this repulſion ſeems to begin much ſooner to affect the tail, than the body of the comet; which is ſuppoſed always to

paſs

paſs the ſun before it begins to fly away from him, which is by no means the caſe with the tail. The repulſive force, therefore, (if there is any ſuch) is in a much leſs proportion than the attractive one; and probably juſt only enough to counterbalance the latter, when theſe bodies are in their perihelions, and to turn them ſo much aſide, as to prevent their falling into the body of the ſun. The projectile force they have acquired will then carry them out to the heavens; and repulſion probably diminiſhing as they recede from the ſun's atmoſphere, his attraction will again take place, and retard their motion regularly, till they arrive at their aphelia, when they once more begin to return to him.

I don't know how you will like all this: —Our comet has led me a dance I very little thought of; and I believe I ſhould have done better to ſend it at once into the ſun, and had done with it: and that, indeed,

indeed, I am apt to believe, will be its fate. For as this comet has no tail, there is, of consequence, no apparent repulsion. If it was repelled, its atmosphere, like the others, would be driven away in the opposite direction from the sun; I therefore do not see any possible method it has of escaping.

These comets are certainly bodies of a very different nature from those with tails, to which indeed they appear even to bear a much less resemblance than they do to planets: and it is no small proof of the little progress we have made in the knowledge of the universe, that they have not as yet been distinguished by a different name.

This is the third kind of body that has been discovered in our system, that all appear essentially different from each other, that are probably regulated by different laws, and intended for very different purposes.

poses.—How much will posterity be astonished at our ignorance, and wonder that this system should have existed for so many thousand years, before we were in the least acquainted with one half of it, or had even invented names to distinguish its different members!

I have no doubt, that in future ages, the number of the comets, the form of their orbits, and time of their revolutions, will be as clearly demonstrated as that of the planets. It is our countryman, Dr. Halley, who has begun this great work, which may be considered just now as in its earliest infancy.—These bodies too, with thick atmospheres, but without tails, will likewise have their proper places ascertained, and will no longer be confounded with bodies to which they bear no resemblance or connection.

Comets with tails have ſeldom been viſible, but on their receſs from the ſun. It is he that kindles them up, and gives them that alarming appearance in the heavens. —On the contrary, thoſe without tails have ſeldom, perhaps never, been obſerved, but on their approach to him. I don't recollect any whoſe return has been tolerably well aſcertained. I remember, indeed, a few years ago, a ſmall one, that was ſaid to have been diſcovered by a teleſcope, after it had paſſed the ſun, but never more became viſible to the naked eye. This aſſertion is eaſily made, and nobody can contradict it; but it does not at all appear probable, that it ſhould have been ſo much leſs luminous after it had paſſed the ſun, than before it approached him; and I will own to you, when I have heard that the return of theſe comets had eſcaped the eyes of the moſt acute aſtronomers, I have been tempted to think, that they did not return at all, but were abſorbed in the body of the

the ſun, which their violent motion towards him ſeemed to indicate.—Indeed, I have often wiſhed that this diſcovery might be made, as it would in ſome meaſure account for what has as yet been looked upon as unaccountable: that the ſun, notwithſtanding his daily waſte, from enlightening the univerſe, never appears diminiſhed either in ſize or light.—Surely this waſte muſt be immenſe, and were there not in nature ſome hidden proviſion for ſupplying it, in the ſpace of ſix thouſand years, ſuppoſing the world to be no older, the planets muſt have got to a much greater diſtance from his body, by the vaſt diminution of his attraction; they muſt likewiſe have moved much ſlower, and conſequently the length of our year muſt have been greatly increaſed.—Nothing of all this ſeems to be the caſe: the diameter of the ſun is the ſame that ever it was: he neither appears diminiſhed, nor our diſtance from him increaſed: his light, heat,

heat, and attraction seem to be the same as ever; and the motion of the planets round him is performed in the same time; of consequence, his quantity of matter still continues the same.—How then is this vast waste supplied?—May there not be millions of bodies attracted by him, from the boundless regions of space, that are never perceived by us? Comets, on their road to him, have several times been accidentally discovered by telescopes, that were never seen by the naked eye.—Indeed, the number of black spots on the sun seem to indicate that there is always a quantity of matter there, only in a preparation to give light, but not yet refined and pure enough to throw off rays like the rest of his body. For I think we can hardly conceive, that any matter can remain long on the body of the sun without becoming luminous; and so we find these spots often disappear, that is to say, the matter of which they are composed is then perfectly

fectly melted, and has acquired the same degree of heat and light as the rest of his body.—Even in our glass-houses, and other very hot furnaces, most sorts of matter very soon acquire the same colour and appearance as the matter in fusion, and emit rays of light like it. But how much more must this be the case at the surface of the sun! when Newton computes, that even at many thousand miles distance from it, a body would acquire a degree of heat two thousand times greater than that of red hot iron. It has generally been understood, that he said the great comet really did acquire this degree of heat; but this is certainly a mistake: Sir Isaac's expression, to the best of my remembrance, is, that it might have acquired it. And if we consider the very great size of that body, and the short time of its perihelion, the thing will appear impossible: nor indeed do I think we can conceive, that a body only as large as our Earth, and the spots

on

on the ſun are often much larger, could be reduced to fuſion, even on his ſurface, but after a very conſiderable ſpace of time.

Now as it ſeems to be univerſally ſuppoſed, that the rays of light are really particles of matter, proceeding from the body of the ſun, I think it is abſolutely neceſſary that we ſhould fall upon ſome ſuch method of ſending him back a ſupply of thoſe rays, otherwiſe, let his ſtock be ever ſo great, it muſt at laſt be exhauſted.

I wiſh aſtronomers would obſerve whether the ſpots on the ſun are not increaſed after the appearing of theſe comets; and whether theſe ſpots do not diſappear again by degrees, like a body that is gradually melted down in a furnace. But there is another conſideration too, which naturally occurs: pray what becomes of all this vaſt quantity of matter after it is reduced to light?—Is it ever collected again into ſolid bodies; or is it for ever loſt and diſſipated, after it has made its journey from the ſun to the object it illuminates?—It is ſomewhat ſtrange, that of all that immenſe quantity of matter poured down on us during the day, that pervades and fills the whole univerſe; the moment we are deprived of the luminous body, the whole of it, in an inſtant, ſeems to be annihilated: —in ſhort, there are a number of difficulties attending the common received doctrine of light; nor do I think there is any point in natural philoſophy the ſolution of which is leſs ſatisfactory. If we ſuppoſe every ray to be a ſtream of particles of matter, darting from the luminous body, how can we conceive that theſe ſtreams may be interſected and pierced by other ſtreams of the ſame matter ten thouſand thouſand different ways, without cauſing the leaſt confuſion either to the one or the other?

other? for in a clear night we see distinctly any particular star that we look at, although the rays coming from that star to our eye is pierced for millions of miles before it reaches us, by millions of streams of the same rays, from every other sun and star in the universe. Now suppose, in any other matter that we know of, and one would imagine there ought at least to be some sort of analogy; suppose, I say, we should only attempt to make two streams pass one another; water, for instance, or, air, one of the purest and the most fluid substances we are acquainted with, we find it totally impossible.—The two streams will mutually interrupt and incommode one another, and the strongest will ever carry off the weakest into its own direction; but if a stream of light is hit by ten thousand other streams, moving at the rate of ten millions of miles in a minute, it is not even bent by the impression, nor in the smallest degree diverted from its

 course;

course; but reaches us with the same precision and regularity, as if nothing had interfered with it. Besides, on the supposition that light is real particles of matter moving from the sun to the earth, in the space of seven minutes, how comes it to pass, that with all this wonderful velocity, there seems to be no momentum! for it communicates motion to no body that obstructs its passage, and no body whatever is removed by the percussion.— Supposing we had never heard of this discovery, and were at once to be told of a current of matter flying at the rate of ten millions of miles in a minute, and so large as to cover one half of our globe, would we not imagine that the earth must instantly be torn to pieces by it, or carried off with the most incredible velocity? It will be objected, that the extreme minuteness of the particles of light prevents it from having any such effect;—but as these particles are in such quantity, and so close to each other as to cover the ſurface of every body that is oppoſed to them, and entirely to fill up that vaſt ſpace betwixt the earth and the ſun, this objection I ſhould think in a great meaſure falls to the ground. The particles of air and of water are likewiſe extremely minute, and a ſmall quantity of theſe will produce little or no effect, but increaſe their number, and only give them the millionth part of the velocity that is aſcribed to a ray of light, and no force whatever could be able to withſtand them.

Adieu.—I have unwarily run myſelf into the very deeps of philoſophy; and find it rather difficult to ſtruggle out again.—I aſk your pardon, and promiſe, if poſſible, for the future, to ſteer quite clear of them. —I am ſure, whatever this comet may be to the univerſe, it has been an ignis fatuus to me; for it has led me ſtrangely out of my road, and bewildered me amongſt rocks and quickſands, where I was like to ſtick fifty times.

I have forgot whether or not you are a rigid Newtonian; if you are, I believe I had better recant in time, for fear of accidents. I know this is a very tender point; and have ſeen many of thoſe gentlemen, who are good Chriſtians too, that can bear with much more temper to hear the divinity of our Saviour called in queſtion, than that of Sir Iſaac; and look on a Carteſian or a Ptolomean, as a worſe ſpecies of infidel than an atheiſt.

I remember, when I was at college, to have ſeen a heretic to their doctrine of gravity, very ſuddenly converted by being toſſed in a blanket; and another, who denied the law of centripetal and centrifugal forces, ſoon brought to aſſent, from having the demonſtration made upon his ſhoulders, by a ſtone whirled at the end of a ſtring.

These are powerful arguments, and it is difficult to withstand them.—I cry you mercy.—I am without reach of you at present, and you are heartily welcome to wreck your vengeance on my letter.

## LETTER XXVII.

Palermo, July 6th.

MANY of the churches here are extremely rich and magnificent. The cathedral (or, as they call it, *Madre Chiesa*) is a venerable Gothic building, and of a large size; it is supported within by eighty columns of Oriental granite, and divided into a great number of chapels, some of which are extremely rich, particularly that of St. Rosolia, the patroness of Palermo, who is held in greater veneration here, than all the persons of the Trinity; and, which is still much more, than even the Virgin Mary herself. The relics of the saint are preserved in a large box of silver, curiously wrought, and enriched with precious stones. They perform many miracles, and are looked upon as the greatest treasure of the city.

They

They are eſteemed a moſt effectual remedy againſt the plague, and have often preſerved them from that fatal diſtemper. The ſaint gained ſo much credit, in ſaving them from the laſt plague of Meſſina, although it was at two hundred miles diſtance, that they have, out of gratitude, erected a noble monument to her.—St. Agatha did as much for Catania, but that city has not been ſo generous to her.—The other riches of this church conſiſt principally in ſome bones of St. Peter, and a whole arm of St. John the Baptiſt.—There is likewiſe a jaw-bone of prodigious efficacy; and ſome other bones of leſſer note.—It contains ſome things of ſmaller conſequence, which, however, are not altogether without their merit. The monuments of their Norman kings, ſeveral of whom lie buried here, are of the fineſt porphiry, ſome of them near ſeven hundred years old, and yet of very tolerable workmanſhip. Oppoſite to theſe, there is a taber-

tabernacle of lapis lazuli. It is about fifteen feet high, and finely ornamented. Some of the presents made to St. Rosolia, are by no means contemptible. A cross of very large brilliants, from the king of Spain, is, I think, the most considerable.

The Sachristie too is very rich: There are some robes embroidered with Oriental pearl, that are near four hundred years old, and yet look as fresh as if done yesterday.

The Jesuits church is equal in magnificence to any thing I have seen in Italy.— The genius of those fathers appears strong in all their works; one is never at a loss to find them out. They have been grossly calumniated; for they certainly had less hypocrisy than any other order of monks.

The Chiesa del Pallazzo is entirely encrusted over with antient mosaic; and the vaulted roof too is all of the same.—But it is endless to talk of churches. Here are upwards of three hundred.—That of Monreale, about five miles distant from this city, is the next in dignity in the island, after the cathedral of Palermo. It is nearly of the same size, and the whole is encrusted with mosaic, at an incredible expence. Here are likewise several porphiry and marble monuments of the first kings of Sicily. This cathedral was built by King William the Good, whose memory is still held in great veneration amongst the Sicilians.

The archbishop of Monreale, is already looked upon as a saint, and indeed he deserves beatification better, I believe, than most of those in the calendar. His income is very great, of which he reserves to himself just as much as procures him clothes,

clothes, and the simplest kind of food; all the rest he devotes to charitable, pious, and public uses. He even seems to carry this too far, and denies himself the most common gratifications of life. Such as sleeping on a bed; a piece of luxury he is said never to indulge himself in, but lies every night on straw.—He is, as you may believe, adored by the people, who crowd in his way as he passes to receive his benediction; which they allege is even of more sovereign efficacy than that of the pope. And indeed so it is, for he never sees an object in distress, but he is sure to relieve him; not trusting alone to the spiritual efficacy of the blessing, but always accompanying it with something solid and temporal; and perhaps this accompaniment is not esteemed the worst part of it. The town and country round Monreale are greatly indebted to his liberality; and in every corner exhibit marks of his munificence. He has just now made a present to the cathedral of a magnificent altar; only about one half of which is finiſhed. It is of maſſive ſilver, exquiſitely wrought, repreſenting in high relief, ſome of the principal ſtories in the Bible, and, I think, will be one of the fineſt in the world.—But what is of much greater utility, he has at his own expence made a noble walk the whole way from this city to Monreale, which was formerly of very difficult acceſs, as it ſtands near the top of a pretty high mountain. The walk is cut with a great deal of judgment on the ſide of this mountain, and winds by eaſy zig-zags to the top of it. It is adorned with ſeveral elegant fountains of water, and is bordered on each ſide with a variety of flowering ſhrubs.—The valley at the foot of the mountain is rich and beautiful. It appears one continued orange garden for many miles, and exhibits an elegant piece of ſcenery; perfuming the air at the ſame time with the moſt delicious odours.—We were ſo pleaſed with this little expedition, that notwithſtanding the heat of the ſeaſon, we could not keep in our carriage, but walked almoſt the whole of it.

The city of Palermo for theſe ten days paſt has been wholly occupied in preparing for the great feaſt of St. Roſolia. And if the ſhew is in any degree adequate to the expence and trouble it coſts them, it muſt indeed be a very noble one. They are erecting an incredible number of arches and pyramids for the illuminations. They are of wood; painted, and adorned with artificial flowers. Theſe, they tell us, are to be entirely covered over with ſmall lamps; ſo that when ſeen at a little diſtance, they appear like ſo many pyramids and arches of flame. The whole Marino, and the two great ſtreets that divide the city, are to be illuminated in this magnificent manner. The number of pyramids and arches prepared for theſe illuminations, we are told, exceeds two thousand. They are erected on each side of the street, betwixt the foot-path and the pavement, and run in two right lines exactly parallel from end to end. Each of these lines is a mile in length, which makes four miles for the whole. The four gates are the vistas to these four streets, and are to be highly decorated and illuminated. From the square in the center of the city, the whole of this vast illumination can be seen at once; and they assure us the grandeur of it exceeds all belief.—The whole of the Marino is to be dressed out in the same manner; and for these three weeks past, they have been employed in erecting two great theatres for fireworks. One of these fronts the viceroy's palace, and is almost equal to it in size. The other is raised on piles driven in the sea, exactly opposite to the great orchestra in the center of the Marino.—Besides these, they are building an enormous engine, which they call St. Rosolia's

triumphal

triumphal car. From the ſize of it, one would imagine it were for ever to remain in the ſpot where it is erected; but they aſſure us, it is to be drawn in triumph through the city. It is indeed mounted upon wheels, but it does not appear that any force whatever can be able to turn them.

I own my curioſity increaſes every day to ſee this ſingular exhibition. The car is already higher than moſt houſes in Palermo, and they are ſtill adding to its height. But the part of the ſhew they value themſelves the moſt on, is the illumination of the great church; this they affirm is ſuperior to any thing in the world; the illumination of St. Peter's itſelf not excepted. The preparations for it, are indeed amazing. Theſe were begun about a month ago, and will not be finiſhed till towards the laſt days of the feaſt. The whole of the cathedral, both roof and walls,

walls, is entirely covered over with mirrour, intermixed with gold and silver paper, and an infinite variety of artificial flowers. All theſe are arranged and diſpoſed, in my opinion, with great taſte and elegance; none of them predominate, but they are intermingled every where in a juſt proportion.

Every altar, chapel, and column are finiſhed in the ſame manner, which takes off from the littleneſs of the particular ornaments, and gives an air of grandeur and uniformity to the whole. The roof is hung with innumerable luſtres filled with wax candles, and, I am perſuaded, when the whole is lighted up, it muſt be equal to any palace either in the Fairy Tales or the Arabian Nights Entertainment. Indeed it ſeems pretty much in the ſame ſtile too, for all is gold, ſilver, and precious ſtones. The ſaints are dreſſed out in all their glory, and the fairy queen herſelf was never finer than is St. Rosolia.—The people are lying yonder in crowds before her, praying with all their might.—I dare say, for one petition offered to God Almighty, she has at least an hundred.

We were just now remarking, with how little respect they pass the chapels dedicated to God; they hardly deign to give a little inclination of the head; but when they come near those of their favourite saints, they bow down to the very ground: Ignorance and superstition have ever been inseparable:—I believe in their hearts they think he has already reigned long enough; and would be glad to have a change in the government:—and every one of them (like the poor Welchman who thought he should be succeeded by Sir Watkin Williams) is fully persuaded, that his own favourite saint is the true heir apparent. Indeed they already give them the precedency on most occasions; not in processions and affairs of etiquette; there they think it would not be decent; but, in their more private affairs, they generally pay the compliment to the ſaint:—Yet in their inſcriptions on churches and chapels, (which one would think are public enough) when they are dedicated to God and any particular ſaint, they have often ventured to put the name of the ſaint firſt.—Sancto Januario, et Deo Opt. Max. taking every opportunity of raiſing their dignity, though at the expence of that of God himſelf.

## LETTER XXVIII.

Palermo, July 7th.

I HAVE been enquiring who this ſame St. Roſolia may be, who has become ſo very capital a perſonage in this part of the world; but, notwithſtanding their adoring her with ſuch fervency, I have found none that can give any tolerable account of her ſaintſhip. They refer you to the moſt fabulous legends, that even differ widely in their accounts of her. And, after all the offerings they have made, the churches they have built, and monuments they have raiſed to her memory, I think it is far from being improbable, that there really never did exiſt ſuch a perſon. I went through all the bookſellers ſhops, but could find nothing relative to her, except an epic poem, of which ſhe is the heroine. It is

in

in the Sicilian language; and is indeed one of the greateſt curioſities I have met with. The poet ſets her at once above all other ſaints except the Virgin, and it ſeems to be with the greateſt reluctance, that he can prevail upon himſelf to yield the pas even to her. I find, from this curious compoſition, and the notes upon it, that St. Roſolia was niece to King William the Good. That ſhe began very early to diſplay ſymptoms of her ſanctity. That at fifteen ſhe deſerted the world and diſclaimed all human ſociety. She retired to the mountains on the weſt of this city; and was never more heard of for about five hundred years. She diſappeared in the year 1159. The people thought ſhe had been taken up to heaven; till in the year 1624, during the time of a dreadful plague, a holy man had a viſion, that the ſaint's bones were lying in a cave near the top of the Monte Pelegrino. That if they were taken up with due reverence, and carried in proceſſion thrice round the walls of the city, they ſhould immediately be delivered from the plague. At firſt little attention was paid to the holy man, and he was looked upon as little better than a dreamer; however, he perſiſted in his ſtory, grew noiſy, and got adherents. The magiſtrates, to pacify them, ſent to the Monte Pelegrino; when lo the mighty diſcovery was made! —the ſacred bones were found,—the city was freed from the plague,—and St. Roſolia became the greateſt ſaint in the calendar.—Churches were reared, altars were dedicated, and miniſters appointed to this new divinity, whoſe dignity and conſequence have ever ſince been ſupported at an incredible expence. Now I think it is more than probable that theſe bones, that are now ſo much reverenced, and about which this great city is at preſent in ſuch a buſtle, belong to ſome poor wretch that perhaps was murdered, or died for want in the mountains. The holy man probably could

could have given a very good account of them.

It is really aſtoniſhing to think, what animals ſuperſtition makes of mankind.—I dare ſay, the bones of St. Roſolia are juſt as little intitled to the honours they receive, as thoſe of poor *St. Viar*, which were found ſomewhere in Spain under a broken tomb-ſtone, where theſe were the only legible letters. The ſtory I think, is told by Dr. Middleton. The prieſts found that the bones had an excellent knack at working miracles, and were of opinion that this, together with the *S. Viar* on the ſtone, was proof ſufficient of his ſanctity. He continued long in high eſtimation, and they drew no inconſider-able revenue from his abilities; till unfor-tunately they petitioned the pope to grant him ſome immunities. The pope (Leo the tenth, I think,) not entirely ſatisfied with regard to his ſaintſhip, deſired to be in-formed of his pretenſions.—A liſt of his miracles was ſent over, accompanied by the ſtone with *S. Viar* upon it. The firſt part of the proof was ſuſtained; but the antiquaries diſcovered the fragment to be part of the tomb-ſtone of a (Roman) *præfectus viarum*, or overſeer of the high roads; to whoſe bones they had been ſo much indebted: and poor St. Viar, though probably an honeſter man than moſt of them, was ordered to be ſtruck out of the calendar.

The people of faſhion here hold the ſuperſtition of the vulgar in great contempt; and perhaps that very ſuperſtition is one principal cauſe of their infidelity. Indeed I have ever found, that deiſm is moſt prevalent in thoſe countries where the people are the wildeſt and moſt bigotted.—A refined and cultivated underſtanding, ſhocked at their folly, thinks it cannot poſſibly recede too far from it, and is often tempted to fly to the very oppoſite extreme.—When reaſon is much offended by any particular dogma of faith

faith or act of worship, she is but too apt, in the midst of her disgust, to reject the whole. The great misfortune is, that in these countries, the most violent champions for religion are commonly the most weak and ignorant; —And certainly, one weak advocate in any cause, but more particularly in a mysterious one, that requires to be handled with delicacy and address, is capable of hurting it more, than fifty of its warmest opponents.—Silly books, that have been written by weak well-meaning men, in defence of religion, I am confident have made more infidels than all the works of Bolingbroke, Shaftesbury, or even Voltaire himself: they only want to make people believe that there are some ludicrous things to be said against it; but these grave plodding blockheads do all they can to persuade us that there is little thing to be said for it. —The universal error of these gentry, is that they ever attempt to explain, and reconcile to sense and reason those very mysteries

teries that the firſt principles of our religion teach us are incomprehenſible; and of conſequence neither objects of ſenſe nor reaſon.—I once heard an ignorant prieſt declare, that he did not find the leaſt difficulty, in conceiving the myſtery of the Trinity, or that of incarnation; and that he would undertake to make them plain to the meaneſt capacities. A gentleman preſent told him, he had no doubt he could, to all ſuch capacities as his own. The prieſt took it as a compliment, and made him a bow.—Now don't you think, that a few ſuch teachers as this, muſt hurt religion more by their zeal, than all its opponents can by their wit? Had theſe heroes ſtill kept behind the bulwarks of faith and of myſtery, their adverſaries never could have touched them; but they have been fooliſh enough to abandon theſe ſtrong-holds, and dared them forth to combat on the plain fields of reaſon and of ſenſe.—A ſad piece of generalſhip indeed: ſuch defenders muſt ever ruin the beſt cauſe.

But

But although the people of education here despise the wild superstition of the vulgar, yet they go regularly to mass, and attend the ordinances with great respect and decency; and they are much pleased with us for our conformity to their customs, and for not appearing openly to despise their rites and ceremonies. I own, this attention of theirs, not to offend weak minds, tends much to give us a favorable opinion both of their hearts and understandings. They don't make any boast of their infidelity; neither do they pester you with it as in France, where it is perpetually buzz'd in your ears; and where, although they pretend to believe less, they do in fact believe more than any nation on the continent.

I know of nothing that gives one a worse opinion of a man, than to see him make a shew and parade of his contempt for things held sacred: it is an open insult to the

judgment

judgment of the public. A countryman of ours, about two years ago, offended egregiously in this article, and the people still speak of him both with contempt and detestation. It happened one day, in the great church, during the elevation of the host, when every body else were on their knees, that he still kept standing, without any appearance of respect to the ceremony. A young nobleman that was near him expressed his surprize at this. "It is strange, "Sir, (said he) that you, who have had "the education of a gentleman, and ought "to have the sentiments of one, should "chuse thus to give so very public offence." "Why, Sir, (said the Englishman) I don't "believe in transubstantiation."—"Neither "do I, Sir, (replied the other) and yet you "see I kneel."

Adieu. I am called away to see the preparations for the feast. In my next I shall probably give you some account of it.

P. S. I have been watching with great care the return of our comet, but as yet I have diſcovered nothing of it: I obſerve too, with a very indifferent glaſs, ſeveral large round ſpots on the ſun's diſk, and am far from being certain that it is not one of them: but I ſhall not alarm you any more with this ſubject.

## LETTER XXIX.

Palermo, July 10th.

ON Sunday, the 8th, we had the long expected Sirocc wind, which, although our expectations had been raiſed pretty high, yet I own it greatly exceeded them. Ever ſince we came to our new lodging, the thermometer has ſtood betwixt 72 and 74; at our old one, it was often at 79 and 80; ſo great is the difference betwixt the heart of the city and the ſea-ſhore. At preſent, our windows not only front to the North, but the ſea is immediately under them, from whence we are conſtantly refreſhed by a delightful cooling breeze. Friday and Saturday were uncommonly cool, the mercury never being higher than $72\frac{1}{2}$; and although the Sirocc is ſaid to have ſet in early on Sunday morning, the air in our

apart-

apartments, which are very large, with high cielings, was not in the least affected by it at eight o'clock, when I rose.—I opened the door without having any suspicion of such a change; and indeed I never was more astonished in my life.—The first blast of it on my face felt like the burning steam from the mouth of an oven. I drew back my head and shut the door, calling out to Fullarton, that the whole atmosphere was in a flame. However, we ventured to open another door that leads to a cool platform, where we usually walk; this was not exposed to the wind; and here I found the heat much more supportable than I could have expected from the first specimen I had of it at the other door. It felt somewhat like the subterraneous sweating stoves at Naples; but still much hotter.—In a few minutes we found every fibre greatly relaxed, and the pores opened to such a degree, that we expected soon to be thrown into a profuse sweat. I went to examine the thermometer, and found the air in the room as yet ſo little affected, that it ſtood only at 73. The preceding night it was at $72\frac{1}{2}$. I took it out to the open air, when it immediately roſe to 110, and ſoon after to 112; and I am confident, that in our old lodgings, or any where within the city, it muſt have riſen ſeveral degrees higher. The air was thick and heavy, but the barometer was little affected; it had fallen only about a line. The ſun did not once appear the whole day, otherwiſe I am perſuaded the heat muſt have been inſupportable; on that ſide of our platform which is expoſed to the wind, it was with difficulty we could bear it for a few minutes. Here I expoſed a little pomatum which was melted down, as if I had laid it before the fire. I attempted to take a walk in the ſtreet, to ſee if any creature was ſtirring, but I found it too much for me, and was glad to get up ſtairs again.

This extraordinary heat continued till 3 o'clock in the afternoon, when the wind changed at once, almoſt to the oppoſite point of the compaſs, and all the reſt of the day it blew ſtrong from the ſea. It is impoſſible to conceive the different feeling of the air. Indeed, the ſudden change from heat to cold is almoſt as inconceivable as that from cold to heat. The current of this hot air had been flying for many hours from South to North; and I had no doubt, that the atmoſphere, for many miles round, was entirely compoſed of it; however, the wind no ſooner changed to the North, than it felt extremely cold, and we were ſoon obliged to put on our clothes, for till then we had been almoſt naked. In a ſhort time the thermometer ſunk to 82, a degree of heat that in England would be thought almoſt inſupportable, and yet all that night we were obliged, merely from the cold, to keep up the glaſſes of our coach; ſo much were the pores opened and the fibres relaxed by theſe few hours of the Sirocc. Indeed, I had expoſed myſelf a good deal to the open air, as I was determined to feel what effect it would produce on the human body. At firſt I thought it muſt have been impoſſible to bear it; but I ſoon diſcovered my miſtake, and found, that where I was ſheltered from the wind, I could walk about without any great inconveniency; neither did it produce that copious ſweat I expected; it occaſioned indeed a violent perſpiration, which was only attended with a ſlight moiſture on the ſkin; but I ſuppoſe, if I had put on my clothes, or taken the leaſt exerciſe, it ſoon would have brought it on.

I own to you my curioſity with regard to the Sirocc is now thoroughly ſatisfied; nor do I at all wiſh for another viſit of it during our ſtay in Sicily. Many of our acquaintance who had been promiſing us this *regalo*, as they call it, came crowding

about

about us as soon as it was over, to know what we thought of it. They own it has been pretty violent for the time it lasted; but assure us they have felt it more so, and likewise of a much longer duration; however, it seldom lasts more than thirty-six or forty hours, so that the walls of the houses have not time to be heated throughout, otherwise they think there could be no such thing as living: however, from what I felt of it, I believe they are mistaken. Indeed, had I been satisfied with the first blast, (which is generally the case with them) and never more ventured out in it, I certainly should have been of their opinion. They laughed at us for exposing ourselves so long to it; and were surprized that our curiosity should lead us to make experiments at the expence of our persons. They assure us, that during the time it lasts, there is not a mortal to be seen without doors, but those whom necessity obliges. All their doors and windows are shut close, to prevent the external air from entering; and where there are no window-ſhutters, they hang up wet blankets on the inſide of the window. The ſervants are conſtantly employed in ſprinkling water through their apartments, to preſerve the air in as temperate a ſtate as poſſible; and this is no difficult matter here, as I am told there is not a houſe in the city that has not a fountain within it. By theſe means the people of faſhion ſuffer very little from the Sirocc, except the ſtrict confinement to which it obliges them.

It is ſomewhat ſingular, that notwithſtanding the ſcorching heat of this wind, it has never been known to produce any epidemical diſtempers, nor indeed bad conſequences of any kind to the health of the people. It is true, they feel extremely weak and relaxed during the time it blows, but a few hours of the Tramontane, or North wind, which generally ſucceeds it, ſoon

braces

braces them up, and ſets them to rights again. Now, in Naples, and in many other places in Italy, where its violence is not to be compared to this, it is often attended with putrid diſorders, and ſeldom fails to produce almoſt a general dejection of ſpirits. It is true, indeed, that there the Sirocc laſts for many days, nay, even for weeks; ſo that, as its effects are different, it probably proceeds likewiſe from a different cauſe.

I have not been able to procure any good account of this very ſingular object in the climate of Palermo. The cauſes they aſſign for it are various, though none of them, I think, altogether ſatisfactory.

I have ſeen an old fellow here, who has written upon it. He ſays it is the ſame wind that is ſo dreadful in the ſandy deſarts of Africa, where it ſometimes proves mortal in the ſpaçe of half an hour. He alleges that it is cooled by its paſſage over the ſea, which entirely diſarms it of theſe tremendous effects, before it reaches Sicily. But if this were true, we ſhould expect to find it moſt violent on that ſide of the Iſland that lies neareſt to Africa, which is not the caſe:—though indeed it is poſſible, that its heat may be again increaſed by its paſſage acroſs the iſland; for it has ever been found much more violent at Palermo, which is near the moſt northern point, than any where elſe in Sicily.—Indeed, I begin to be more reconciled to this reaſon, when I conſider that this city is almoſt ſurrounded by high mountains, the ravines and vallies betwixt which are parched up and burning hot at this ſeaſon. Theſe likewiſe contain innumerable ſprings of warm water, the ſteams of which muſt tend greatly to increaſe the heat, and perhaps likewiſe to ſoften the air, and diſarm it of its noxious qualities. It is a practice too, at this ſeaſon, to burn heath and bruſhwood on the mountains,

tains, which muſt ſtill add to the heat of the air.

Some gentlemen who were in the country told me, that they walked out immediately after the Sirocc, and found the graſs and plants, that had been green the day before, were become quite brown, and crackled under their feet as if dried in an oven.

I ſhall add for your amuſement, a journal of the weather ſince we came to Palermo. The barometer has continued conſtantly within a line or two of the ſame point, $29\frac{1}{2}$;—and the ſky has been always clear, except the day of the Sirocc and the 26th of June, when we had a pretty ſmart ſhower of rain for two hours; ſo that I think I have nothing farther to do, but to mark the heights of the thermometer.

| | Thermometer. |
|---|---|
| June 17 - - - - | $73\frac{1}{2}$ |
| 18 - - | 74 |

| | | Thermometer. |
|---|---|---|
| June 19 | - - | 75 |
| 20 | | 76 |
| 21 | - - | $75\frac{1}{2}$ |
| 22 | | 77 |
| 23 | | $76\frac{1}{2}$ |
| 24 | | 77 |
| 25 | | 77 |
| 26 | | $77\frac{1}{2}$ |
| 27 | - | 77 |
| 28 | | $77\frac{1}{2}$ |
| 29 | - | $77\frac{1}{2}$ |
| 30 | | $78\frac{1}{2}$ |
| July 1 | | 79 |
| 2 | | 80 |
| 3 | - - - | $80\frac{1}{2}$ |
| 4 | At our new lodgings on the ſea-ſide, fronting the North, | 74 |
| 5 | - - - | 73 |
| 6 | - - | $72\frac{1}{2}$ |
| 7 | - - - | $72\frac{1}{2}$ |
| 8 | The Sírocc wind, - | 112 |
| | In the afternoon, | 82 |
| 9 | - - - | 79 |
| 10 | - - | 78 |

The

The more I consider the extreme violence of this heat, the more I am surprised that we were able to bear it with so little inconvenience. We did not even feel that depression of spirits that commonly attends very great heats with us.—The thermometer rose 40 degrees, or very near it; and it happens singularly enough, that before the Sirocc began, it stood just about 40 degrees above the point of congelation; so that in the morning of the 8th of July, the heat increased as much, almost instantaneously, as it generally does during the whole time that the sun moves from tropic to tropic; for the difference of 72 and 112 is the same as between the freezing point and 72; or between a cold day in winter, and a warm one in summer.

Yesterday we had a great entertainment in the palace of the Prince Partana, from the balcony of which the viceroy reviewed a regiment of Swiss, the best I have yet seen

ſeen in the Neapolitan ſervice. They are really a fine body of men, and, notwithſtanding the violence of the heat, went through their motions with great ſpirit. They had two field-pieces on each flank, which were extremely well ſerved; and the evolutions were performed with more preciſion and ſteadineſs than one generally meets with, except in England or Germany. The grenadiers were furniſhed with falſe grenades, which produced every effect of real ones, except that of doing miſchief. The throwing of theſe was the part of the entertainment that ſeemed to pleaſe the moſt; and the grenadiers took care to direct them ſo, that their effect ſhould not be loſt. When a number of them fell together amongſt a thick crowd of the nobility, which was commonly the caſe, it afforded an entertaining ſcene enough, for they defended themſelves with their hats, and threw them very dexterouſly upon their neighbours. However, we ſaw no damage done, except the singeing of a few wigs and caps; for the ladies were there in as great numbers as the gentlemen.

The company at the Prince Partana's was brilliant, and the entertainment noble. It consisted principally of ices, creams, chocolate, sweet-meats, and fruit, of which there was a great variety. Not one half of the company play'd at cards; the rest amused themselves in conversation and walking on the terrass. We found the young prince and princess, who are very amiable, with several of their companions playing at cross-purposes, and other games of that kind. We were joyfully admitted of this chearful little circle, where we amused ourselves very well for several hours.—I only mention this, to shew you the different system of behaviour here and in Italy, where no such familiar intercourse is allowed amongst young people before marriage. The young ladies here are easy, affable,

affable, and unaffected; and, not (as on the continent) perpetually ſtuck up by the ſides of their mothers, who bring them into company, not for their amuſement, but rather to offer them to ſale; and ſeem mightily afraid leſt every one ſhould ſteal them, or that they themſelves ſhould make an elopement; which indeed I ſhould think there was ſome danger of, conſidering the reſtraint under which they are kept:—for ſurely there is no ſuch ſtrong incitement to vice, as the making a puniſhment of virtue.

Here the mothers ſhew a proper confidence in their daughters, and allow their real characters to form and to ripen. In the other caſe they have either no character at all, or an affected one, which they take care to throw off the moment they have got a huſband; when they think it impoſſible to recede too far from thoſe rigorous maxims of decorum and circumſpection, the practice

practice of which they had ever found so extremely disagreeable.

Were they allowed first to shew what they really are, I am persuaded they would not be half so bad; but their parents, by the manner they treat them, shew that they have no confidence in their principles; and seem to have adopted the ungenerous maxim of our countryman,

"That every woman is at heart a rake."

Now in countries where this maxim becomes of general belief, there is no doubt, that it likewise becomes true; for the women having no longer any character to support, they will even avoid the pretences to virtue, well knowing that those pretences are only looked upon as hypocrisy and affectation. I dare say, you will agree with me, that the better method to make them virtuous, is first to make them believe that we think them so; for where virtue is really

esteemed,

esteemed, there are none that would willingly relinquish the character; but where it requires a guard, (as parson Adams says) it certainly is not worth the centinel.

Some of the families here put me in mind of our own domestic system. The prince of Resuttana, his wife and daughter, are always together; but it is because they chuse to be so, and there appears the strongest affection, without the least diffidence on the one side, or restraint on the other.—The young princess Donna Rosolia is one of the most amiable young ladies I have seen; she was of our little party last night, and indeed made one of its greatest ornaments.—It would appear vain and partial, after this to say, that in countenance, sentiment, and behaviour, she seems altogether English;—bnt it is true:—and this perhaps may have contributed to advance her still higher in our esteem; for in spite of all our philosophy, these unphilosophical prejudices

judices will ſtill exiſt, and no man, I believe, has entirely diveſted himſelf of them. —We had lately a noble entertainment at her father's country houſe, and had reaſon to be much pleaſed with the unaffected hoſpitality and eaſy politeneſs of the whole family. This palace is reckoned the moſt magnificent in the neighbourhood of Palermo. It lies about ſix or ſeven miles to the weſt of the city, in the country called Il Colle; in the oppoſite direction from the Bagaria, which I have already mentioned. The viceroy and his family, with the greateſt part of the nobility, were of this party, which laſted till about two in the morning. At midnight a curious ſet of fire-works were played off, from the leads of the palace, which had a fine effect from the garden below.

Farewell.—I had no time to write yeſterday, and though we did not break up till near three this morning, I have got up at at eight, I was ſo eager to give you ſome account of the Sirocc wind.

We are now going to be very buſy: The feaſt of St. Roſolia begins to-morrow; and all the world are on the very tip-toe of expectation: perhaps they may be diſappointed. I often wiſh that you were with us, particularly when we are happy: Though you know it is by no means feaſts and ſhews that make us ſo. However, as this is perhaps the moſt remarkable one in Europe; that you may enjoy as much of it as poſſible, I ſhall ſit down every night, and give you a ſhort account of the tranſactions of the day.—We are now going to breakfaſt; after which we are engaged to play at Ballon, an exerciſe I ſuppoſe you are well acquainted with; but as the day promiſes to be extremely hot, I believe I ſhall deſert the party and go a ſwimming.—But I ſee F. and G. have already attacked the figs and peaches, ſo I muſt appear for my intereſt.—Farewell.

## LETTER XXX.

Palermo, July 12th.

ABOUT five in the afternoon, the festival began by the triumph of St. Rosolia, who was drawn with great pomp through the center of the city, from the Marino to the Porto Nuovo. The triumphal car was preceded by a troop of horse, with trumpets and kettle-drums; and all the city officers in their gala uniforms. It is indeed a most enormous machine: It measures seventy feet long, thirty wide, and upwards of eighty high; and, as it passed along, over-topped the loftiest houses of Palermo. The form of its under-part is like that of the Roman gallies, but it swells as it advances in height; and the front assumes an oval shape like an amphi-

 theatre,

theatre, with ſeats placed in the theatrical manner. This is the great orcheſtra, which was filled with a numerous band of muſicians placed in rows, one above the other: Over this orcheſtra, and a little behind it, there is a large dome ſupported by ſix Corinthian columns, and adorned with a number of figures of ſaints and angels; and on the ſummit of the dome there is a gigantic ſilver ſtatue of St. Roſolia.—The whole machine is dreſſed out with orange-trees, flower-pots, and trees of artificial coral. The car ſtopped every fifty or ſixty yards, when the orcheſtra performed a piece of muſic, with ſongs in honour of the ſaint. It appeared a moving caſtle, and completely filled the great ſtreet from ſide to ſide. This indeed was its greateſt diſadvantage, for the ſpace it had to move in was in no wiſe proportioned to its ſize, and the houſes ſeemed to dwindle away to nothing as it paſſed along. This vaſt fabric was drawn by fifty-ſix huge

mules,

mules, in two rows, curiously caparisoned, and mounted by twenty-eight postilions, dressed in gold and silver stuffs, with great plumes of ostrich feathers in their hats.— Every window and balcony, on both sides of the street, were full of well-dressed people, and the car was followed by many thousands of the lower sort. The triumph was finished in about three hours; and was succeeded by the beautiful illumination of the Marino.

I believe I have already mentioned, that there is a range of arches and pyramids extending from end to end of this noble walk: these are painted, and adorned with artificial flowers, and are entirely covered with lamps, placed so very thick, that at a little distance the whole appears so many pyramids and arches of flame. The whole chain of this illumination was about a mile in length, and indeed you can hardly conceive any thing more splendid. There was no break or imperfection any where; the night being so still that not a single lamp was extinguished.

Opposite to the center of this great line of light, there was a magnificent pavilion erected for the viceroy and his company, which consisted of the whole nobility of Palermo: and on the front of this, at some little distance in the sea, stood the great fire-works, representing the front of a palace, adorned with columns, arches, trophies, and every ornament of architecture. All the chebecks, galleys, galliots, and other shipping, were ranged around this palace, and formed a kind of amphitheatre in the sea, inclosing it in the center.—These began the shew by a discharge of the whole of their artillery, the sound of which, re-echoed from the mountains, produced a very noble effect; they then played off a variety of water rockets, and bombs of a curious construction, that often burst below water. This continued for half an hour, when, in an instant, the whole of the palace was beautifully illuminated. This was the signal for the shipping to cease, and appeared indeed like a piece of inchantment, as it was done altogether instantaneously, and without the appearance of any agent. At the same time the fountains that were represented in the court before the palace, began to spout up fire, and made a representation of some of the great *jet d'eaus* of Versailles and Marly. As soon as these were extinguished, the court assumed the form of a great parterre; adorned with a variety of palm-trees of fire, interspersed with orange-trees, flower-pots, vases, and other ornaments. On the extinguishing of these, the illumination of the palace was likewise extinguished; and the front of it broke out into the appearance of a variety of suns, stars, and wheels of fire, which in a short time reduced it to a perfect ruin.

And when all appeared finiſhed, there burſt from the center of the pile, a vaſt exploſion of two thouſand rockets, bombs, ſerpents, ſquibs, and devils, which ſeemed to fill the whole atmoſphere; the fall of theſe made terrible havoc amongſt the clothes of the poor people who were not under cover, but afforded admirable entertainment to the nobility who were. During this exhibition we had a handſome entertainment of coffee, ices and ſweetmeats, with a variety of excellent wines, in the great pavilion in the center of the Marino; this was at the expence of the Duke of Caſtellano, the prætor (or mayor) of the city. The principal nobility give theſe entertainments by turns every night during the feſtival, and vie with each other in their magnificence.

As ſoon as the fireworks were finiſhed, the viceroy went out to ſea in a galley richly illuminated. We choſe to ſtay on shore, to see the appearance it made at a distance. It was rowed by seventy-two oars, and indeed made one of the most beautiful objects you can imagine; flying with vast velocity over the waters, as smooth and as clear as glass, which shone round it like a flame, and reflected its splendour on all sides. The oars beat time to the French-horns, clarionets, and trumpets, of which there was a numerous band on the prow.

The day's entertainment was concluded by the Corso, which began exactly at midnight, and lasted till two in the morning.

The great street was illuminated in the same magnificent manner as the Marino. The arches and pyramids were erected at little distances from each other, on both sides of the street, betwixt the foot-path and the space for carriages; and when seen from either of the gates, appeared to be two continued lines of the brighteſt flame. Indeed, theſe illuminations are ſo very different, and ſo much ſuperior, to any I have ever ſeen, that I find it difficult to give any tolerable idea of them.—Two lines of coaches occupied the ſpace betwixt theſe two lines of illumination. They were in their greateſt gala; and as they open from the middle, and let down on each ſide, the beauty of the ladies, the richneſs of their dreſs, and brilliance of their jewels, were diſplayed in the moſt advantageous manner.

This beautiful train moved ſlowly round and round for the ſpace of two hours; and every member of it ſeemed animated with a deſire to pleaſe.—The company appeared all joy and exultation:—Scarce two coaches paſſed without ſome mutual acknowledgment of affection or reſpect; and the pleaſure that ſparkled from every eye ſeemed to be reflected and communicated by by a kind of ſympathy through the whole.

In ſuch an aſſembly, it was impoſſible for the heart not to dilate and expand itſelf;—I own mine was often ſo full, that I could hardly find utterance; and I have ſeen a tragedy with leſs emotion than I did this ſcene of joy.—I always thought theſe affections had been ſtrangers to pomp and parade; but here the univerſal joy ſeemed really to ſpring from the heart: it brightened up every countenance, and ſpoke affection and friendſhip from every face.—No ſtately air,—no ſupercilious look;—all appeared friends and equals.—And ſure I am, that the beauty of the ladies was not half ſo much heightened either by their dreſs or their jewels, as by that air of complacency and good humour with which it was animated.

We

We were distributed in different coaches amongst the nobility, which gave us a better opportunity of making these observations.—I will own to you, that I have never beheld a more delightful sight;—and if superstition often produces such effects, I sincerely wish we had a little more of it amongst us. I could have thrown myself down before St. Rosolia, and blessed her for making so many people happy.

We retired about two o'clock; but the variety of glittering scenes and gaudy objects still vibrated before my eyes, and prevented me from sleeping; however, I am almost as much refreshed as if I had: but I really believe four more such days will be too much for any of us. Indeed, I am sure that it is impossible to keep it up, and it must necessarily flag. I think, from what I can observe, they have already exhausted almost one half of their preparations;

rations; how they are to support the other four days, I own, I do not comprehend;—however, we shall see.

I thought to have given you an account of every thing at night, after it was over, but I find it impossible: the spirits are too much dissipated, and exhausted, and the imagination is too full of objects to be able to separate them with any degree of regularity.—I shall write you therefore regularly the morning following, when this fever of the fancy has had time to cool, and when things appear as they really are.—Adieu then till to-morrow.—Here is a fine shower, which will cool the air, and save the trouble of watering the Marino and the great street, which is done regularly every morning when there is no rain. The thermometer is at 73.

13th. I thought there would be a falling off.—Yesterday's entertainments were not

not so splendid as those of the day before. They began by the horse-races. There were three races, and six horses started each race. These were mounted by boys of about twelve years old, without either saddle or bridle, but only a small piece of cord, by way of bit, in the horse's mouth, which it seems is sufficient to stop them. The great street was the course; and to this end it was covered with earth to the depth of five or six inches.—The firing of a cannon at the Porto Felice was the signal for starting; and the horses seemed to understand this, for they all set off at once, full speed, and continued at their utmost stretch to the Porto Nuovo, which was the winning post. It is exactly a mile, and they performed it in a minute and thirty-five seconds; which, considering the size of the horses, (scarce fourteen hands) we thought was very great. These are generally Barbs, or a mixed breed, betwixt the Sicilian and Barb. The boys were gaudily

dressed,

dreſſed, and made a pretty appearance.—We were ſurpriſed to ſee how well they ſtuck on; but indeed, I obſerved they had generally laid faſt hold of the mane.

The moment before ſtarting, the ſtreet appeared full of people; nor did we conceive how the race could poſſibly be performed. Our ſurpriſe was increaſed when we ſaw the horſes run full ſpeed at the very thickeſt of this crowd, which did not begin to open, till they were almoſt cloſe upon it.—The people then opened, and fell back on each ſide, by a regular uniform motion, from one end of the ſtreet to the other. This ſingular manœuvre ſeemed to be performed without any buſtle or confuſion, and the moment the horſes were paſt, they cloſed again behind them. However, it deſtroys great part of the pleaſure of the race; for you cannot help being under apprehenſions for ſuch a number of people, whom you every moment ſee

in

in imminent danger of being trod to death; for this must inevitably be their fate, were they only a second or two later in retiring. These accidents, they allow, have often happened; however, yesterday every body escaped.

The victor was conducted along the street in triumph, with his prize displayed before him. This was a piece of white silk embroidered and worked with gold.

These races I think are much superior to the common stile of races in Italy, which are performed by horses alone without riders; but they are by no means to be compared to those in England.

The great street was illuminated in the same manner as on the preceding night; and the grand conversation of the nobles was held at the archbishop's palace, which was richly fitted up for the occasion.

The

The gardens were finely illuminated; and put me in mind of our Vauxhall. There were two orchestras (one at each end) and two very good bands of music. The entertainment was splendid, and the archbishop shewed attention and politeness to every person of the company.

About ten o'clock the great triumphal car marched back again in procession to the Marino. It was richly illuminated with large wax tapers, and made a most formidable figure.—Don Quixote would have been very excusable in taking it for an inchanted castle, moving through the air.—We did not leave the archbishop's till midnight, when the Corso began, which was precisely the same in every respect as the night before, and afforded us a delightful scene.

14th. Last night the two great streets and the four gates of the city that terminate

minate them, were illuminated in the most splendid manner.—These streets cross each other in the center of the city, where they form a beautiful square, called *La Piazza Ottangolare*, from the eight angles they form. This square was richly ornamented with tapestry, statues, and artificial flowers; and as the buildings which form its four sides are uniform, and of a beautiful architecture, and at the same time highly illuminated, it made a fine appearance. There are four orchestras erected in it; and the four bands of music are greater than I had any conception this city could have produced.

From the center of this square you have a view of the whole city of Palermo thus dressed out in its glory; and indeed, the effect it produces surpasses belief. The four gates that form the vistas to this splendid scene are highly decorated, and lighted up in an elegant taste; the illu-

minations

minations repreſenting a variety of trophies, the arms of Spain, thoſe of Naples, Sicily, and the city of Palermo, with their guardian geniuſes, &c.

The converſation of the nobles was held in the viceroy's palace; and the entertainment was ſtill more magnificent than any of the former. The great fireworks oppoſite to the front of the palace began at ten o'clock, and ended at midnight; after which we went to the Corſo, which laſted, as uſual, till two in the morning. This part of the entertainment ſtill pleaſes us the moſt; it is indeed the only part of it that reaches the heart; and where this is not the caſe, a puppet-ſhew is juſt as good as a coronation.—We have now got acquainted almoſt with every countenance; and from that air of goodneſs and benignity that animates them, and which ſeems to be mutually reflected from one to the other, we are inclined to form the most favourable opinion of the people.

Our fireworks last night were greater than those of the Marino, but their effect did not please me so much; the want of the sea and the shipping were two capital wants. They likewise represented the front of a palace, but of a greater extent. It was illuminated too as the former, and the whole conducted pretty much in the same manner. We saw it to the greatest advantage from the balconies of the state apartments, in the viceroy's palace, where we had an elegant concert; but, to the no small disappointment of the company, Gabrieli, the finest singer, but the most capricious mortal upon earth, did not chuse to perform.

15th. Three races, six horses each, as formerly. They called it very good sport. I cannot say that I admired it.—A poor

creature

creature was rode down, and I believe killed; and one of the boys had likewise a fall.

The great aſſembly of the nobility was held at the Judice Monarchia's, an officer of high truſt and dignity. Here we had an entertainment in the ſame ſtile as the others, and a good concert.—At eleven o'clock the viceroy, attended by the whole company, went on foot to viſit the ſquare and the great church.—We made a prodigious train; for though the city was all a lamp of light, the ſervants of the viceroy and nobility attended with wax flambeaux, to ſhew us the way. As ſoon as the viceroy entered the ſquare, the four orcheſtras ſtruck up a ſymphony, and continued playing till he left it.

The crowd around the church was very great, and without the preſence of the viceroy, it would have been impoſſible for us to get in: but his attendants ſoon cleared the paſſages; and at once entering the great gate, we beheld the moſt ſplendid ſcene in the world. The whole church appeared a flame of light; which, reflected from ten thouſand bright and ſhining ſurfaces, of different colours and at different angles, produced an effect, which, I think, exceeds all the deſcriptions of enchantment I have ever read. Indeed, I did not think that human art could have deviſed any thing ſo ſplendid. I believe I have already mentioned that the whole church, walls, roof, pillars, and pilaſters were entirely covered over with mirror, interſperſed with gold and ſilver paper, artificial flowers, &c. done up with great taſte and elegance, ſo that not one inch either of ſtone or plaiſter was to be ſeen.—Now, form an idea, if you can, of one of our great cathedrals dreſſed out in this manner, and illuminated with twenty thouſand wax tapers, and you will have ſome faint notion

 of

of this ſplendid ſcene.—I own it did greatly exceed my expectations, although, from the deſcriptions we had of it, they were raiſed very high.—When we recovered from our firſt ſurprize, which had produced, unknown to ourſelves, many exclamations of aſtoniſhment, I obſerved that all the eyes of the nobility were fixed upon us; and that they enjoyed exceedingly the amazement into which we were thrown.—Indeed this ſcene, in my opinion, greatly exceeds all the reſt of the ſhew.

I have often heard the illumination of St. Peter's ſpoken of as a wonderful fine thing: ſo indeed it is; but it is certainly no more to be compared to this, than the planet Venus is to the ſun.—The effects indeed are of a different kind, and cannot well be compared together.

This ſcene was too glaring to bear any conſiderable time; and the heat occaſioned

 by

by the immenſe number of lights, ſoon became intolerable.—I attempted to reckon the number of luſtres, and counted upwards of five hundred; but my head became giddy, and I was obliged to give it up.—They aſſure us that the number of wax tapers is not leſs than twenty thouſand. There are eight-and-twenty altars, fourteen on each ſide; theſe are dreſſed out with the utmoſt magnificence; and the great altar is ſtill the moſt ſplendid of all.

When you think of the gaudy materials that compoſe the lining of this church, it will be difficult to annex an idea of grandeur and majeſty to it: at leaſt, ſo it ſtruck me, when I was firſt told of it; yet, I aſſure you, the elegant ſimplicity and unity of the deſign prevents this effect, and gives an air of dignity to the whole.

It

It is on this part of the ſhew the people of Palermo value themſelves the moſt; they talk of all the reſt as trifling in compariſon of this; and indeed, I think it is probable, that there is nothing of the kind in the world that is equal to it.—It is ſtrange they ſhould chuſe to be at ſo great an expence and trouble, for a ſhew of a few hours only; for they have already begun this morning, to ſtrip the church of its gaudy dreſs, and I am told it will not be finiſhed for many weeks.

From the church we went immediately to the Corſo, which concluded, as uſual, the entertainments of the day.

16th. Laſt night we had the full illumination of all the ſtreets.—The aſſembly was held at the prætor's, where there was an elegant entertainment and a concert.—Pacherotti, the firſt man of the opera, diſtinguiſhed himſelf very much. I think he is one of the moſt agreeable ſingers I have ever heard; and am perſuaded, that in a few years, he will be very celebrated. Campanucci, the ſecond ſoprano, is, I think, preferable to moſt that I have heard in Italy; and you will the more eaſily believe this, when I inform you, that he is engaged for next winter, to be the firſt ſinger in the great opera at Rome. Is it not ſtrange, that the capital of all Italy; and, for the fine arts, (as it formerly was for arms) the capital of the world, ſhould condeſcend to chuſe its firſt opera-performer from amongſt the ſubalterns of a remote Sicilian ſtage?

You will believe, that with two ſuch ſopranos as theſe, and Gabrieli for the firſt woman, the opera here will not be a deſpicable one. It is to begin in a few days, notwithſtanding the extreme heat of the ſeaſon; ſo fond are the people here of theſe entertainments.

Their opera dancers are thoſe you had laſt year at London: they are juſt arrived, and the people are by no means pleaſed with them. We ſaw them this morning at the rehearſal; and, to their great ſurprize, addreſſed them in Engliſh. You cannot imagine how happy they were to ſee us. Poor ſouls! I was delighted to hear with what warmth of gratitude and affection they ſpoke of England. There is a mother and two daughters; the youngeſt pretty, but the eldeſt, the firſt dancer, appears a ſenſible, modeſt, well-behaved girl;—more ſo than is common with theſe ſort of people. Speaking of England, ſhe ſaid, with a degree of warmth, that her good treatment in general could hardly inſpire, that in her life ſhe never left any country with ſo ſore a heart; and had ſhe only enjoyed her health, all the world ſhould never have torn her away from it.—She ſeemed affected when ſhe ſaid this.—I acknowledged

the

the honour ſhe did the Engliſh nation; but alleged that theſe ſentiments, and the manner in which they were uttered, could ſcarcely proceed from a *general love* of the country.—She anſwered me with a ſmile, but at the ſame time I could obſerve the tear in her eye.—At that inſtant we were interrupted; however, I ſhall endeavour, if poſſible, to learn her ſtory; for I am perſuaded there is one: perhaps you may know it, as I dare ſay it is no ſecret in London.

But I have got quite away from my ſubject, and had forgot that I ſat down to give you an account of the feaſt.—Indeed, I will own, it is a kind of ſubject I by no means like to write upon;—I almoſt repent that I had undertaken it, and am heartily glad it is now over.—It does very well to ſee ſhews; but their deſcription is of all things on earth the moſt inſipid: for words and writing convey

ideas

ideas only by a slow and regular kind of progreſs; and while we gain one, we generally loſe another, ſo that the fancy ſeldom embraces the whole;—but when a thouſand objects ſtrike you at once, the imagination is filled and ſatisfied.

The great proceſſion that cloſes the feſtival began at ten o'clock.—It only differed from other proceſſions in this, that beſides all the prieſts, friars, and religious orders of the city, there were placed at equal diſtances from each other ten lofty machines made of wood and paſteboard, ornamented in an elegant manner, repreſenting temples, tabernacles, and a variety of beautiful pieces of architecture.—Theſe are furniſhed by the different convents and religious fraternities, who vie with each other in the richneſs and elegance of the work. Some of them are not leſs than ſixty feet high.—They are filled with figures

figures of ſaints and of angels, made of wax, ſo natural and ſo admirably well painted, that many of them ſeemed really to be alive. All theſe figures are prepared by the nuns, and by them dreſſed out in rich robes of gold and ſilver tiſſue.

We were a good deal amuſed this morning to ſee them returning home in coaches to their reſpective nunneries.—At firſt we took them for ladies in their gala dreſs, going out to viſit the churches, which we were told was the cuſtom, and began to pull off our hats as they went paſt.—Indeed, we were led into this blunder by ſome of our friends, who carried us out on purpoſe; and as they ſaw the coaches approach, told us, This is the Princeſs of ſuch a thing—there is the Dutcheſs of ſuch another thing;—and, in ſhort, we had made half a dozen of our beſt bows, (to the no ſmall entertainment of theſe wags) before we discovered the trick —They now insist upon it, that we are good Catholics, for all this morning we have been bowing to saints and angels.

A great silver box, containing the bones of St. Rosolia, closed the procession. It was carried by thirty-six of the most respectable burgesses of the city, who look upon this as the greatest honour. The archbishop walked behind it, giving his benediction to the people as he passed.

No sooner had the procession finished the tour of the great square, before the prætor's palace, than the fountain in the center, one of the largest and finest in Europe, was converted into a fountain of fire; throwing it up on all sides, and making a beautiful appearance. It only lasted for a few minutes, and was extinguished by a vast explosion, which concluded the whole. As this was altogether unex-

unexpected, it produced a fine effect, and surprised the spectators more than any of the great fireworks had done.

There was a mutual and friendly congratulation ran through the whole assembly, which soon after parted; and this morning every thing has once more reassumed its natural form and order;—and I assure you, we were not more happy at the opening of the festival, than we are now, at its conclusion. Every body was fatigued and exhausted by the perpetual feasting, watching, and dissipation of these five days. However, upon the whole, we have been much delighted with it, and may with truth pronounce, that the entertainments of the feast of St. Rosolia are much beyond those of the holy week at Rome; of the Ascension, at Venice; or, indeed, any other festival we have ever been witness of.



I believe

I believe I did not tell you, that about ten or twelve days ago, as the time we had appointed for our return to Naples was elapſed, we had hired a ſmall veſſel, and provided every thing for our departure: we had even taken leave of the viceroy, and received our paſſports. Our baggage and ſea-ſtore was already on board, when we were ſet upon by our friends, and ſolicited with ſo much earneſtneſs and cordiality, to give them another fortnight, that we found it impoſſible to refuſe it; and in conſequence diſcharged our veſſel, and ſent for our trunks.—I ſhould not have mentioned this, were it not to ſhew you how much more attention is paid to ſtrangers here than in moſt places on the continent.

We reckon ourſelves much indebted to them for having obliged us to prolong our ſtay; as, independent of the amuſements of the feſtival, we have met with ſo much hoſpi-

hoſpitality and urbanity, that it is now with the moſt ſincere regret we find ourſelves obliged to leave them. Indeed, had we brought our clothes and books from Naples, it is hard to ſay how long we might have ſtayed.

We have ſent to engage a veſſel, but probably ſhall not ſail for five or ſix days. Adieu.

## LETTER XXXI.

Palermo, July 19th.

WE have now had time to enquire a little into ſome of the antiquities of this iſland, and have found ſeveral people, particularly the prince of Torremuzzo, who have made this the great object of their ſtudy. However, I find we muſt wade through oceans of fiction, before we can arrive at any thing certain or ſatiſfactory.

Moſt of the Sicilian authors agree in deriving their origin from Ham, or as they call him, Cham, the ſon of Noah, who, they pretend, is the ſame with Saturn. They tell you that he built a great city, which from him was named Cameſena. There have been violent diſputes about the

 ſituation

ſituation of this city:—Beroſo ſuppoſes it to have ſtood, where Camarina was afterwards founded, and that this was only a corruption of its primitive name. But Guarneri, Carrera, and others, combat this opinion, and affirm, that Cameſena ſtood near the foot of Ætna, between Aci and Cattania, almoſt oppoſite to theſe three rocks that ſtill bear the name of the Cyclops.—Indeed Carrera mentions an inſcription that he had ſeen in a ruin near Aci, ſuppoſed to have been the ſepulchre of Acis, which he thinks puts this matter out of doubt. Theſe are his words: "Hæc eſt inſcriptio vetuſtæ cujuſdam tabellæ repertæ in pyramide ſepulchri Acis, ex fragmentis vetuſtiſſimæ Chameſenæ, urbis hodie Acis, conditæ a Cham, gigantum principe, etiam nuncupato Saturno Chameſeno, in promontorio Xiphonio, ubi adhuc hodie viſuntur ſolo æquata antiqua veſtigia, et ruinæ dictæ urbis et arcis in inſula prope Scopulos Cyclopum,

Cyclopum, et retinet adhuc sindopatum nomen La Gazzena."

This ſame Cham they tell you was a very great ſcoundrel, and that *eſenus*, which ſignified infamous, was added to his name, only to denote his character. Fazzello ſays, he married his own ſiſter, who was called Rhea; that Ceres was the fruit of this marriage; that ſhe did not inherit the vices of her father, but reigned over Sicily with great wiſdom and moderation. That ſhe taught her ſubjects the method of making bread and wine, the materials for which their iſland produced ſpontaneouſly in great abundance. That her daughter Proſerpine was of equal beauty and virtue with herſelf. That Orius king of Epirus had demanded her in marriage, and on a refuſal, carried her off by force; which gave occaſion to the wild imagination of Greece to invent the fable of the rape of Proſerpine by Pluto king of Hell, this

Orius being of a moroſe and gloomy diſpoſition.

Ceres has ever been the favourite deity of the Sicilians. She choſe her ſeat of empire in the center of the iſland, on the top of a high hill called Enna, where ſhe founded the city of that name. It is ſtill a conſiderable place, and is now called Caſtragiovanni; but little or nothing remain of the ruins of Enna.

Cicero gives a particular account of this place. He ſays, from its ſituation in the center of the iſland, it was called *Umbilicus Siciliæ*, and deſcribes it as one of the moſt beautiful and fertile ſpots in the world. The temple of Ceres at Enna was renowned all over the heathen world, and pilgrimages were made to it, as they are at preſent to Loretto. Fazzello ſays, it was held in ſuch veneration, that when the city was ſurprized and pillaged by the ſlaves and barbarians,

barians, they did not preſume to touch this ſacred temple, although it contained more riches than all the city beſides.

There have been violent diſputes amongſt the Sicilian authors, whether Proſerpine was carried off near the city of Enna, or that of Ætna, which ſtood at the foot of that mountain, but it is of mighty little conſequence, and more reſpect, I think, is to be paid to the ſentiments of Cicero, who gives it in favour of Enna, than the whole of them. Diodorus too is of the ſame opinion, and his deſcription of this place is almoſt in the very words as that of Cicero. They both paint it as a perfect paradiſe; abounding in beautiful groves, clear ſprings and rivulets, and like Ætna, covered with a variety of flowers at all ſeaſons of the year. To theſe authorities, if you pleaſe you may add that of Milton, who compares it to paradiſe itſelf.

——Nor that fair field
Of Enna, where Proserpine gathering flowers,
Herself a fairer flower, by gloomy Dis
Was gathered.

If you want to have a fuller account of this place you will find it in Cicero's pleadings against Verres, and in the fifth book of Diodorus.—I have conversed with several gentlemen who have been there: they assure me that it still answers in a great measure to the description of these authors.—Medals, I am told, are still found, with an elegant figure of Ceres, and an ear of wheat for the reverse; but I have not been able to procure any of them.

There was another temple in Sicily not less celebrated than this one of Ceres.—It was dedicated to Venus Erecina, and, like the other too, was built on the summit of a high mountain. The antient name of this mountain was Eryx, or as the Sicilians

cilians call it Erice, but it is now called St. Juliano. Both mountain and temple are often mentioned by the Greek and Latin hiſtorians, and happily the Sicilian ones have no diſpute about its ſituation or origin, which they make to be almoſt as antient as that of Ceres.—Diodorus ſays, that Dedalus, after his flight from Crete, was hoſpitably received here, and by his wonderful ſkill in architecture added greatly to the beauty of this temple. He enriched it with many fine pieces of ſculpture, but particularly with the figure of a ram of ſuch exquiſite workmanſhip that it appeared to be alive. This, I think, is likewiſe mentioned by Cicero.

Æneas too in his voyage from Troy to Italy, landed in this part of the iſland, and according to Diodorus and Thucydides, made rich preſents to this temple; but Virgil is not ſatisfied with this; he muſt raiſe the piety of his hero ſtill higher, and,

 in

in oppoſition to all the hiſtorians, makes Æneas the founder of the temple *. Its fame and glory continued to increaſe for many ages; and it was ſtill held in greater veneration by the Romans, than it had been by the Greeks. Fazzello ſays, and quotes the authority of Strabo, that ſeventeen cities of Sicily were laid under tribute, to raiſe a ſufficient revenue to ſupport the dignity, and enormous expences of this temple. Two hundred ſoldiers were appointed for its guard, and the number of its prieſts, prieſteſſes, and miniſters male and female, were incredible.

At certain ſeaſons of the year, great numbers of pigeons, which were ſuppoſed to be the attendants of Venus, uſed to paſs betwixt Africa and Italy; and reſting for

* Tum vicina aſtris Erycino in vertice ſede.
Fundatur Veneri Idaliæ, tumuloque ſacerdos
Et lucus late ſacer additur Anchiſaæo.

ſome

ſome days on mount Eryx, and round this temple, it was then imagined by the people that the goddeſs herſelf was there in perſon; and on theſe occaſions, he ſays, they worſhipped her with all their might. —Feſtivals were inſtituted in honour of the deity, and the moſt modeſt woman was only looked upon as a prude, that refuſed to comply with the rites. However, there were not many complaints of this kind; and it has been alleged, that the ladies of Eryx were ſometimes ſeen looking out for the pigeons long before they arrived; and that they uſed to ſcatter peas about the temple to make them ſtay as long as poſſible.

Venus was ſucceeded in her poſſeſſions of Eryx by St. Juliano, who now gives his name both to the city and mountain; and indeed he has a very good title, for when the place was cloſely beſieged, the Sicilians tell you, he appeared on the walls armed

cap-

cap-a-pie, and frightened the enemy to ſuch a degree, that they inſtantly took to their heels, and left him ever ſince in quiet poſſeſſion of it.—It would have been long before Venus and her pigeons could have done as much for them.

Many medals are found in the neighbourhood, but there is not the leaſt veſtige of this celebrated temple.—Some marbles with inſcriptions and engravings that have been found deep below ground are almoſt the only remaining monuments of its exiſtence. Suetonius ſays, that it had even fallen to ruins before the time of Tiberius; but as Venus was the favourite divinity of that emperor, he had ordered it to be magnificently repaired: however, it is ſomewhat difficult to reconcile this with Strabo's account; who tells us, that even before his time it had been totally abandoned; and indeed this ſeems moſt probable, as every veſtige of it has now diſappeared,

peared, which is not commonly the case with the great works of the age of Tiberius.

Æneas landed at the port of Drepanum, at the foot of this mountain. Here he lost his father Anchises; in honour of whom, on his return from Carthage about a year after, he celebrated the games that make so great a figure in the Æneid, which Virgil introduces with a good deal of address as a compliment to the piety of Augustus, who had instituted games of the same kind in honour of Julius Cæsar, his father by adoption.

It is singular, that Virgil's account of this part of Sicily should be so very different from that of Homer, when there was so short a space, only a few months, between the times that their two heroes visited it.—Indeed, Virgil seems to have followed

lowed the hiſtorians, in his conduct of this part of his poem, more than the ſentiments of Homer; who makes this very country where Æneas was ſo hoſpitably received, the habitation of Polyphemus and the Cyclops, where Ulyſſes loſt ſo many of his companions, and himſelf made ſo very narrow an eſcape. The iſland of Licoſia where he moored his fleet, lay very near the port of Drepanum, and Homer deſcribes the adventure of Polyphemus to have happened on the ſhore of Sicily, oppoſite to that iſland. Virgil has taken the liberty to change the ſcene of action, as he was better acquainted both with the geography and hiſtory of the country than Homer; and perhaps with a good deal of propriety places it at the foot of mount Ætna. I am afraid there is not ſo much propriety in his changing the action itſelf, and contradicting the account that Homer gives of it. For Ulyſſes ſays that Polyphemus devoured four of his companions; but that he, by his address, saved all the rest, and was himself the last that escaped out of the cave. Now Virgil makes Ulysses to have told a lie, for he affirms that he left Achemenides behind him; and Achemenides too gives a different account of this affair from Ulysses: he assures Æneas, that Polyphemus devoured only two of his companions; after which they put out his eye, (*acuto telo*) with a sharp weapon; which rather gives the idea of a spear or javelin, than that of a great beam of wood made red hot in the fire, as Homer describes it. But there are many such passages.—Don't you think they seem either to indicate a negligence in Virgil, or a want of deference for his master? neither of which, I believe, he has ever been accused of.

The Sicilian authors are by no means pleased with Virgil for making Æneas the founder

founder of this temple of Venus Erecina. They will only allow that the colony which he was obliged to leave there, after the burning of his ships, did, in honour of his mother Venus, build the city of Eryx around her temple; but they all insist upon it, that the temple was built by Eryx, or as they call him Erice, another son of Venus, but much older than Æneas; the same that was found to be so equal a match for Hercules, but was at last killed by him, at a boxing match near the foot of this mountain. The spot where this is supposed to have happened, still retains the name of *(il campo di Hercole)* the field of Hercules. Through the whole fifth book of the Æneid, this Eryx is stiled the brother of Æneas; and, in his account of the games, Virgil introduces those very gauntlets with which he fought with Hercules, *(in hoc ipso littore)* In this very field. The sight of which, from their enormous ſize, aſtoniſhes the whole hoſt, and frightens the champion Dares ſo much that he refuſes to fight.

Adieu. The opera begins in two days; after which, I think, we ſhall ſoon take leave of Sicily.

Ever your's.

## LETTER XXXII.

Palermo, July 21st.

YESTERDAY we walked up to the Monte Pelegrino to pay our reſpects to St. Roſolia, and thank her for the variety of entertainment ſhe has afforded us. It is one of the moſt fatiguing expeditions I ever made in my life. The mountain is extremely high, and ſo uncommonly ſteep, that the road up to it is very properly termed *la Scala*, or the Stair: before the diſcovery of St. Roſolia, it was looked upon as almoſt inacceſſible, but they have now at a vaſt expence cut out a road, over precipices that were almoſt perpendicular. We found the ſaint lying in her grotto, in the very ſame attitude in which ſhe is ſaid to have been diſcovered; her head reclining gently upon her hand, and a crucifix before her. This is a ſtatue of the fineſt white

marble;

marble, and of moſt exquiſite workmanſhip. It is placed in the inner part of the cavern, on the very ſame ſpot where St. Roſolia expired. It is the figure of a lovely young girl of about fifteen, in an act of devotion. The artiſt has found means to throw ſomething that is extremely touching, into the countenance and air of this beautiful ſtatue. I never in my life ſaw one that affected me ſo much, and am not ſurpriſed that it ſhould have captivated the hearts of the people. It is covered with a robe of beaten gold, and is adorned with ſome valuable jewels. The cave is of a conſiderable extent, and extremely damp, ſo that the poor little ſaint muſt have had very cold uncomfortable quarters. They have built a church around it; and appointed prieſts to watch over theſe precious relics, and receive the offerings of pilgrims that viſit them.

An inſcription graved by the hand of St. Roſolia herſelf, was found in a cave in mount Queſquina, at a conſiderable diſtance from this mountain. It is ſaid that ſhe was diſturbed in her retreat there, and had wandered from thence to mount Pelegrino, as a more retired and inacceſſible place. I ſhall copy it exactly, as it is preſerved in the poor little ſaint's own Latin.

EGO ROSOLIA
SINIBALDI QUISQUI-
NE ET ROSARUM
DOMINI FILIA AMORE
DEI MEI JESU
CHRISTI
IN HOC
ANTRO HABITA-
RI DECREVI.

After St. Roſolia was ſcared from the cave where this inſcription was found, ſhe was never more heard of, till her bones were found about five hundred years after, in this ſpot.

The proſpect from the top of mount Pelegrino is beautiful and extenſive. Moſt of the Lipari iſlands are diſcovered in a very clear day, and likewiſe a large portion of mount Ætna, although at the diſtance of almoſt the whole length of Sicily. The Bagaria too, and the Colle, covered over with a number of fine country houſes and gardens, make a beautiful appearance. The city of Palermo ſtands within leſs than two miles of the foot of the mountain, and is ſeen to great advantage. Many people went to this mountain during the time of the great illumination, from whence they pretend it has a fine effect; but this unfortunately we neglected.

Near the middle of the mountain, and not far from its ſummit, there ſtill appears ſome remains of a celebrated caſtle, the origin of which the Sicilian authors carry back to the moſt remote antiquity. Maſſa ſays, it is ſuppoſed to have been built in the reign of Saturn immediately after the flood; for in the time of the earlieſt Carthaginian wars, it was already much reſpected on account of its venerable antiquity.—It was then a place of ſtrength, and is often mentioned by the Greek hiſtorians. Diodorus ſays, in his twenty-third book, that Hamilcar kept poſſeſſion of it for three years, againſt all the power of the Romans; who, with an army of forty thouſand men, attempted in vain to diſlodge him.

The ſituation of Palermo is ſeen, I think, to more advantage from the Monte Pelegrino than from any where elſe. This beautiful city ſtands near the extremity of a kind of natural amphitheatre, formed by high and rocky mountains; but the country that lies betwixt the city and theſe mountains, is one of the richeſt and moſt beautiful ſpots in the world. The whole appears a magnificent garden, filled with fruit-trees of every ſpecies, and watered by clear fountains and rivulets, that form a variety of windings through this delightful plain.—From the ſingularity of this ſituation, as well as from the richneſs of the ſoil, Palermo has had many flattering epithets bestowed upon it; particularly by the poets, who have denominated it *Conca d'oro*, The Golden Shell, which is at once expressive both of its situation and richness. It has likewise been stiled *Aurea Valle*, *Hortus Siciliæ*, &c.; and to include all these together, the lasting term of *Felix* has been added to its name, by which you will find it distinguished even in the maps.

Many of the etymologists allege, that it is from the richness of this valley that it had its original name of *Panormus*, which, in the old Greek language, they pretend, signified All a garden: but others say there is no occasion for straining significations, and assert, with more appearance of plausibility, that it was called *Pan-ormus*, from the size and conveniency of its harbours; one of which is recorded antiently to have extended into the very center of the city. And this is the account Diodorus gives of it; it was called Panormus, ſays he, becauſe its harbour even penetrated to the very innermoſt parts of the city, Panormus in the Greek language ſignifying All a port: And Procopius, in his hiſtory of the wars of the Goths, aſſures us, that in the time of Beliſarius, the port was deep enough for that general to run his ſhips up to the very walls of the city, and give the aſſault from them. It is not now ſo well intitled to this name as it was formerly. Theſe harbours have been almoſt entirely deſtroyed and filled up; moſt probably I think by the violent torrents from the mountains that ſurround it; which are recorded ſometimes to have laid waſte great part of the city. Fazzello ſpeaks of an inundation of which he was an eye-witneſs, that came down from the mountains with ſuch fury, that they thought the city would have been entirely ſwept away. He ſays, it burſt down the wall near to the royal palace, and bore away every thing that oppoſed its paſſage; churches,

churches, convents, houſes, to the number of two thouſand, and drowned upwards of three thouſand people.—Now the fragments and ruins carried to the ſea by ſuch a torrent alone would be ſufficient to fill up a little harbour, ſo that we are not to be ſurpriſed, that theſe capacious ports, for which it had been ſo much celebrated, no longer exiſt.

Next to Chameſeno, Palermo is generally ſuppoſed to be the moſt ancient city in the iſland. Indeed, there ſtill remain ſome monuments that carry back its origin to the times of the moſt remote antiquity. A biſhop of Lucera has wrote on this ſubject. He is clearly of opinion, that Palermo was founded in the days of the firſt patriarchs. You will laugh at this;—ſo did I;—but the biſhop does not go to work upon conjecture only: he ſupports his opinion with ſuch proofs, as I own to you, ſtaggered me a good deal. A Chaldean inſcription was diſcovered about ſix hundred years ago, on a block of white marble; it was in the reign of William II. who ordered it to be tranſlated into Latin and Italian. The biſhop ſays there are many fragments in Palermo with broken inſcriptions in this language; and ſeems to think it beyond a doubt, that the city was founded by the Chaldeans, in the very early ages of the world. This is the literal tranſlation:——"During the time that Iſaac, "the ſon of Abraham, reigned in the valley "of Damaſcus, and Eſau, the ſon of Iſaac, "in Idumea, a great multitude of Hebrews, "accompanied by many of the people of "Damaſcus, and many Phœnicians, coming "into this triangular iſland, took up their "habitation in this moſt beautiful place, "to which they gave the name of Panor-"mus."

The biſhop tranſlates another Chaldean inſcription, which is indeed a great curio-

ſity,

fity. It is still preserved, though not with that care that so valuable a monument of antiquity deserves. It is placed over one of the old gates of the city, and when that gate falls to ruin, it will probably be for ever lost. The translation is in Latin, but I shall give it you in English:——"There "is no other God but one God. There is "no other power but this same God. There "is no other conqueror but this God whom "we adore. The commander of this tower "is Saphu, the son of Eliphar, son of Esau, "brother of Jacob, son of Isaac, son of "Abraham. The name of the tower is "Baych, and the name of the neighbour-"ing tower is Pharat."

These two inscriptions seem to reflect a mutual light upon each other. Fazzello has preserved them both, and remarks upon this last, that it appears evidently from it, that the tower of Baych was built antecedent to the time of Saphu, (or, as we translate

late it, Zephu) who is only mentioned as commander of the tower, but not as its founder,

Part of the ruins of this tower ſtill remain, and many more Chaldean inſcriptions have been found amongſt them, but ſo broken and mangled, that little could be made of them. Fazzello is in great indignation at ſome maſons he found demoliſhing theſe precious relics, and complains bitterly of it to the ſenate, whom he with juſtice upbraids for their negligence and indifference.

Converſing on this ſubject t'other night with a gentleman who is well verſed in the antiquities of this place, I took the liberty of objecting to the Greek etymology, Pan-ormus, it appearing extremely abſurd to give a Greek name to the city long before the exiſtence of the Greek nation: I added, that I was a good deal ſurpriſed

ſurpriſed Fazzello had not attempted to account for this ſeeming abſurdity. He allowed the apparent validity of the objection, and blamed Fazzello for his negligence; but aſſured me, that Pan-ormus, or ſomething very nearly of the ſame ſound, ſignified in the Chaldean language, and likewiſe in the Hebrew, a paradiſe, or delicious garden; and that the Greeks probably finding it ſo applicable, never thought of changing its name. This I was in no capacity to contradict.—He added too, that Panormus was likewiſe an Arabic word, and ſignified *This water*; which probably was the reaſon that the Saracens did not change its name, as they have done that of almoſt every thing elſe; as this is as applicable and as expreſſive of the ſituation of Palermo, as any of the other etymologies; it being ſurrounded on all ſides with beautiful fountains of the pureſt water, the natural conſequence of the vicinity of the mountains.

Pray

Pray ſhew this letter to our friend Mr. Crofts, and deſire his ſentiments on theſe etymologies and antiquities. Tell him I have not forgot his commiſſion, and ſhall procure him all the oldeſt and moſt unintelligible books in Palermo; but I muſt beg, for the repoſe and tranquillity of mankind, that he will not republiſh them. On theſe conditions, I ſend him a moſt valuable fragment: it is part of a Chaldean inſcription that has been exactly copied from a block of white marble found in the ruins of the tower Baych.—I own I ſhould like much to ſee it tranſlated: the people here have as yet made nothing of it: and we were in no capacity to aſſiſt them.

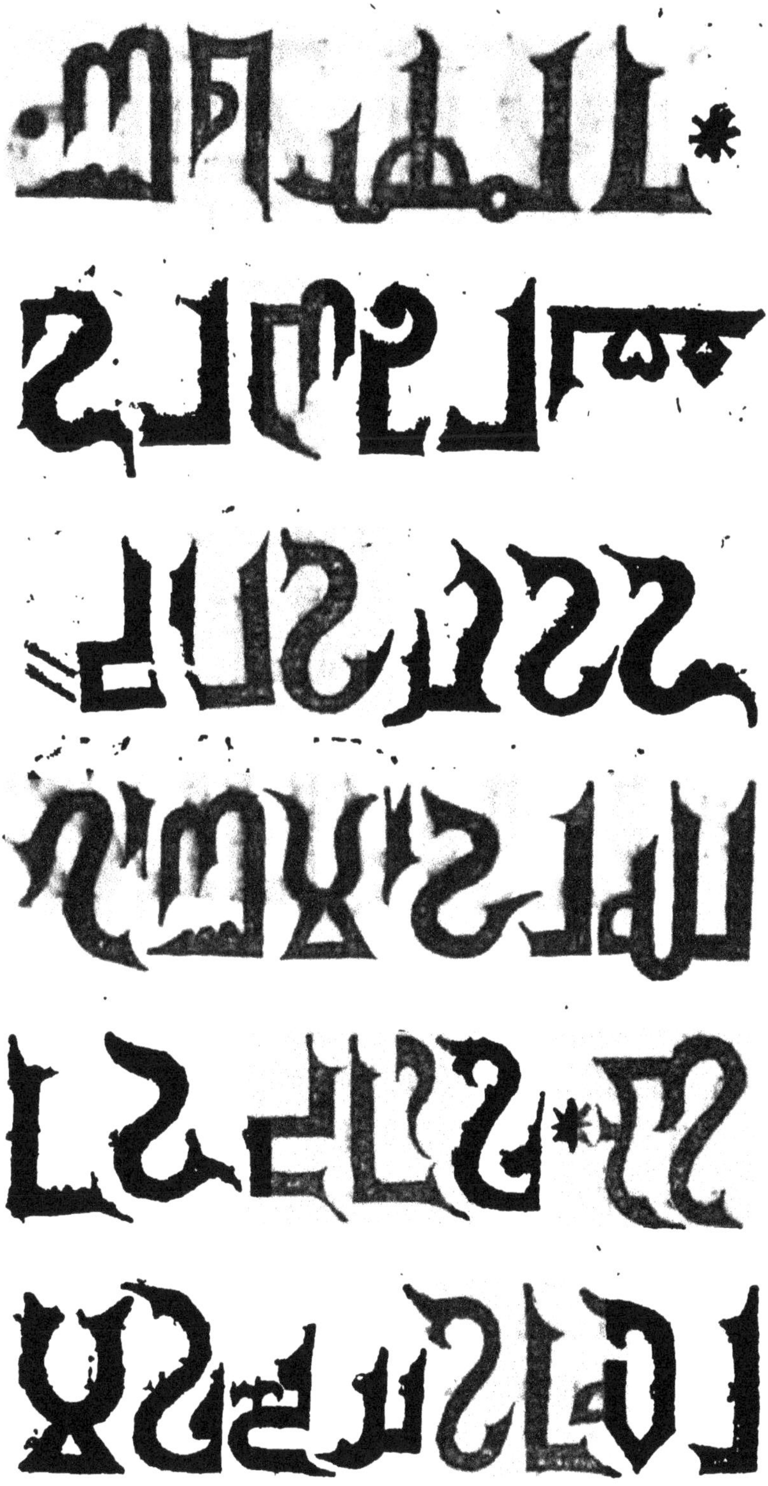

On consulting the Bible, I find, that in our translation, this son of Esau is called Eliphaz, and Eliphaz' son, who was captain of this tower, Zepho. The variation of the names you see is but trifling. It is not improbable that the other tower, Pharat, by a small variation of the same kind, has

has been named from their couſin, Pharez, the ſon of Judah, who got the ſtart of his brother Zarah. You will find the ſtory at the end of the thirty-eighth chapter of Geneſis. The thirty-ſeventh chapter will give you ſome account of Eliphar and [illegible] but I can find no etymology for the name of the tower Baych. I dare ſay Mr. Crofts can tell you what it means.—Pharez ſignifies a breach; a very inauſpicious name one would think for a tower. Adieu. The weather has become exceedingly hot. The thermometer is at 80.

Ever your's.

## LETTER XXXIII.

Palermo, July 24th.

IN the courſe of our acquaintance with ſome gentlemen of ſenſe and obſervation in this place, we have learned many things concerning the iſland, that perhaps may be worthy of your attention; and as this day is ſo hot that I cannot go out, I ſhall endeavour to recollect ſome of them, both for your amuſement and my own. The thermometer is up at 81½.—So you may judge of the ſituation of our northern conſtitutions.

There is one thing, however, that I have always obſerved in theſe ſouthern climates; that although the degree of heat is much greater than with us, yet it is not commonly attended with that weight

and

and oppreſſion of ſpirits that generally accompany our ſultry days in ſummer.—I am ſure, that in ſuch a day as this, in England, we ſhould be panting for breath; and no mortal would think either of reading or writing.—That is not the caſe here; I never was in better ſpirits in my life: Indeed I believe the quantities of ice we eat may contribute a good deal towards it; for I find, that in a very violent heat, there is no ſuch cordial to the ſpirits as ice, or a draught of ice-water: it is not only from the cold it communicates, but, like the cold bath, from the ſuddenneſs of that communication, it braces the ſtomach, and gives a new tone to the fibres.—It is ſtrange that this piece of luxury (in my opinion the greateſt of all, and perhaps the only healthy one) ſhould ſtill be ſo much neglected with us.

I knew an Engliſh lady at Nice, who in a ſhort time was cured of a threatening consumption, only by a free indulgence in the use of ices; and I am persuaded, that in skilful hands, few remedies would be more effectual in many of our stomach and inflammatory complaints, as hardly any thing has a stronger or more immediate effect upon the whole frame; and surely our administering of warm drinks and potions in these complaints tend often to nourish the disease.—It is the common practice here, in inflammatory fevers, to give quantities of ice-water to drink; nay, so far have they carried it, that Dr. Sanghes, a celebrated Sicilian physician, covered over the breast and belly of his patients with snow or ice; and they assure us, in many cases, with great success.—But, indeed, I ought in justice to add, that this physician's practice has not been generally adopted.

Perhaps it is from the present benefit I find from ice, that I have said so much in

favour

favour of it; for I am fully perſuaded, that if I had not a quantity of it ſtanding here below the table, I ſhould very ſoon be obliged to give up writing, and go to bed; but whenever I begin to flag, another glaſs is ſure to ſet me to rights again.

I was going to give you ſome account of the fiſheries of this iſland.

The catching the tunny-fiſh conſtitutes one of the principal Sicilian amuſements during the ſummer months; and the curing and ſending them to foreign markets makes one of the greateſt branches of their commerce.—We were invited yeſterday by the Prince Sperlinga to a party of tunny-fiſhing; but the violence of the heat prevented it.

Theſe fiſh do not make their appearance in the Sicilian ſeas till towards the latter end of May; at which time, the *Tonnaros*, as they call them, are prepared for their reception. This is a kind of aquatic caſtle, formed, at a great expence, of ſtrong nets, faſtened to the bottom of the ſea by anchors and heavy leaden weights.

Theſe tonnaros are erected in the paſſages amongſt the rocks and iſlands that are moſt frequented by the tunny-fiſh. They take care to ſhut up with nets the entry into theſe paſſages, all but one little opening, which is called the outward gate of the tonnaro. This leads into the firſt apartment, or, as they call it, the hall. As ſoon as the fiſh have got into the hall, the fiſhermen, who ſtand ſentry in their boats during the ſeaſon, ſhut the outer door, which is no more than letting down a ſmall piece of net, which effectually prevents the tunny from returning by the way they came. They then open the inner door of the hall, which leads to the ſecond apartment, which they call the antichamber,

chamber, and, by making a noise on the surface of the water, they soon drive the tunny-fish into it. As soon as the whole have got into the antichamber, the inner door of the hall is again shut, and the outer door is opened for the reception of more company.

Some tonnaros have a great number of apartments, with different names to them all; the saloon, the parlour, the dining-room, &c.; but the last apartment is always stiled *la Camera della Morte*, The chamber of Death: this is composed of stronger nets and heavier anchors than the others.

As soon as they have collected a sufficient number of tunny-fish, they are driven from all the other apartments into the chamber of death; when the slaughter begins. The fishermen, and often the gentlemen too, armed with a kind of spear or harpoon, attack the poor defenceleſs animals on all ſides; which now giving themſelves up to deſpair, daſh about with great force and agility, throwing the water over all the boats; and tearing the nets to pieces, they often knock out their brains againſt the rocks or anchors, and ſometimes even againſt the boats of their enemies.

You ſee there is nothing very generous or manly in this ſport.—The taking of the *Peſce Spada*, or ſword-fiſh, is a much more noble diverſion: no art is made uſe of to enſnare him; but with a ſmall harpoon, fixed to a long line, they attack him in the open ſeas, and will often ſtrike him at a very conſiderable diſtance. It is exactly the whale-fiſhing in miniature. The Sicilian fiſhermen (who are abundantly ſuperſtitious) have a Greek ſentence which they make uſe of as a charm to bring him near their boats. This is the only bait they use, and they pretend that it is of wonderful efficacy, and absolutely obliges him to follow them; but if unfortunately he should overhear them speak a word of Italian, he plunges under water immediately, and will appear no more.

As these fish are commonly of a great size and strength, they will sometimes run for hours after they are struck, and afford excellent sport.—I have seen them with a sword four or five feet long, which gives them a formidable appearance in the water, particularly after they are wounded. The flesh of these animals is excellent; it is more like beef than fish, and the common way of dressing it is in steaks.

The fishing of the *pesce spada* is most considerable in the sea of Messina, where they have likewise great quantities of eels, particularly the *Morena*, so much esteemed amongst the Romans, which I think is indeed the finest fish I ever eat.

But it is not only their large fish that they strike with harpoons; they have the same method of taking mullets, dories, a kind of mackarel, and many other species; but this is always performed in the night. As soon as it is dark, two men get into a small boat; one of them holds a lighted torch over the surface of the water, the other stands with his harpoon ready poised in his hand. The light of the torch soon brings the fish to the surface, when the harpooner immediately strikes them. I have seen great quantities killed in this manner, both here and at Naples. A large fleet of boats employed in this kind of fishing make a beautiful appearance on the water, in a fine summer night.

The coral fishery is chiefly practised at Trapani: they have invented a machine

there,

there, which anſwers the purpoſe much beyond their expectations. This is only a great croſs of wood, to the center of which is fixed a heavy hard ſtone, capable of carrying the croſs to the bottom. Pieces of ſmall net are tied to each limb of the croſs, which is poized horizontally by a rope, and let down into the water. As ſoon as they feel it touch the bottom, the rope is made faſt to the boat. They then row about, all over the coral beds: The conſequence of which is, the great ſtone breaks off the coral from the rocks, and it is immediately entangled in the nets.— Since this invention the coral fiſhery has turned out to conſiderable account.

The people of Trapani are eſteemed the moſt ingenious of the iſland; they are the authors of many uſeful and ornamental inventions. An artiſt there, has lately diſcovered a method of making Cameios, which are a perfect imitation of the antient ones

ones engraved on the onyx. They are done on a kind of hard shell from pastes of the best antiques, and so admirably executed, that it is often difficult to distinguish the antient from the modern. These set in gold, are generally worn as bracelets, and are at present in high estimation amongst the ladies of quality here. Mrs. Hamilton * procured a pair of them last year, and carried them to Naples, where they have been much admired. Commissions were immediately sent over, and the man has now more business than he can manage; however, we have been fortunate enough to procure a few pairs of them for our friends. I have seen cameios that have cost two hundred guineas, that could scarce be distinguished from one of these.

The difficulties under which the poor Sicilians labour, from the extreme oppres-

* Now lady Hamilton.

sion

ſion of their government, obliges them ſometimes to invent branches of commerce that nature ſeems to have denied them, as they are not allowed to enjoy thoſe ſhe has beſtowed.—The ſugar-cane was very much cultivated in this iſland, but the duties impoſed were ſo enormous, that it has been almoſt abandoned.—But their crops of wheat alone, were they under a free government, would ſoon be ſufficient to render this little nation one of the richeſt and moſt flouriſhing in the world; for even in the wretched ſtate of cultivation it is in at preſent, one good crop, I am told, is ſufficient to maintain the iſland for ſeven years. You will be a good deal ſurpriſed, after this, to hear that the exportation of this commodity has been prohibited for theſe ſeveral years paſt; at leaſt to all ſuch as are not able to pay moſt exorbitantly for that privilege. The conſequence is, that corn has become a drug. The common price of the ſalma, which is

two

two loads, was about thirty-one ſhillings; at preſent it is reduced to five ſhillings and ſix-pence, and there is a probability that it will ſtill fall lower.

This crop, which has been very abundant, I am told, in many places they have hardly been at the pains to gather in, as there is little probability of this cruel prohibition being removed. The farmers are already ruined, and the ruin of their maſters muſt inevitably follow. This is the method the miniſtry of Naples, or rather that of Spain, has taken to humble the pride of the Sicilian barons, whoſe power they pretend is ſtill very extenſive, and their juriſdiction abſolute; moſt of them poſſeſſing a right of life and death in their own domain. However, there is a probability that they will ſoon be obliged to relinquiſh their privileges. The complaint is univerſal, and if the miniſtry perſevere in theſe rigorous meaſures, there

 muſt

must either be a revolt, or they must soon be reduced to a state of poverty as well as of servitude. I believe indeed most of them would readily embrace any plausible scheme, to shake off their yoke; as in general they appear to be people of great sensibility, with high notions of honour and liberty.

Talking of the natural riches of their island,—Yes, say they, if these were displayed, you would have reason indeed to speak of them. Take a look of these mountains,—they contain rich veins of every metal, and many of the Roman mines still remain;—but to what end should we explore them?—It is not we that should reap the profit.—Nay, a discovery of any thing very rich might possibly prove the ruin of its possessor.—No,—in our present situation the hidden treasures of the island must ever remain a profound secret.—Were we happy enough to enjoy the blessings of your constitution, you

you might call us rich indeed. Many hidden doors of opulence would then be opened, which now are not even thought of, and we ſhould ſoon re-aſſume our antient name and conſequence; but at preſent we are nothing.

This is the language that ſome of the firſt people amongſt them hold with us. However, they ſtill boaſt that they retain more of the feudal government than any nation in Europe. The ſhadow indeed remains, but the ſubſtance is gone long ago. It has long been the object of the Bourbon miniſtry to reduce the power of the barons in every kingdom. Richlieu began the ſyſtem in France, and it has ever ſince been proſecuted by his ſucceſſors; its influence has now ſpread over the whole of their poſſeſſions in Europe; of which, as this is the moſt remote, it has likewiſe been the longeſt in reaching it.

The

The foundation of the feudal ſyſtem was firſt laid here by the count Rugeiro, about the middle of the eleventh century, immediately after he had driven the Saracens out of the iſland. He divided Sicily into three parts; the firſt, by conſent of his army, was given to the church; the ſecond he beſtowed upon his officers, and the third he reſerved for himſelf.

Of theſe three branches, or as they call them *Braccios*, (arms) he compoſed his parliament, the form of which remains the ſame to this day. The *Braccio Militare* is compoſed of all the barons of the kingdom, to the number of two hundred and fifty-one, who are ſtill obliged to military ſervice: their chief is the prince Butero, who is hereditary preſident of the parliament; for in conformity to the genius of the feudal government ſome of the great offices are ſtill hereditary. The three archbiſhops, all the biſhops, abbes, priors, and dignified clergy, amounting to near ſeventy, form the *Braccio Eccleſiaſtico*: The archbiſhop of Palermo is their chief. The *Braccio Demaniale* is formed by election, like our houſe of commons: there are forty-three royal cities, ſtiled *Demaniale*, that have a right to elect members. Every houſeholder had a vote in this election. Their chief is the member for Palermo; who is likewiſe prætor (or mayor of the city). He is an officer of the higheſt rank, and his power is very extenſive; inferior only to that of the viceroy; in whoſe abſence, the greateſt part of the authority devolves upon him. He has a company of grenadiers for his body guard; and receives the title of excellency.

The prætor, together with ſix ſenators, who are ſtiled patricians, have the management of the civil government of the city. He is appointed every year, by the king, or by the viceroy, which is the ſame

thing;

thing; for I don't find that the people any longer exercise even the form of giving their votes: so that the very shadow of liberty has now disappeared as well as the substance.—You may judge of the situation of liberty in a kingdom, where all courts civil and criminal are appointed by regal authority, and where all offices are conferred only by the will of the sovereign, and depend entirely upon his caprice.

I own I feel most sincerely for the Sicilians, who, I think, are possessed of many admirable qualities. But the spirit of every nation must infallibly sink, under an oppressive and tyrannical government.—Their spirit however has in a great measure kept them free from one branch of tyranny, the most dreadful of all, that of the inquisition. The kings of Spain wanted to establish it in its full force; but the barons, accustomed to exercise despotic government themselves, could not bear the thoughts

 of

of becoming slaves to a set of ignorant Spanish priests; and, I believe, they took the only way that was left to avoid it. Every inquisitor that pretended to more zeal than they thought became him, was immediately assassinated; particularly if he presumed to interfere with the conduct or sentiments of the nobility. This soon took off the edge of their zeal, and reduced the holy office to a becoming moderation. However, they are extremely circumspect in their conversation about religious matters; and generally advise strangers to be on their guard, as the power of the inquisition, although considerably reduced, is by no means annihilated.

The laws of Sicily are scattered in a great number of volumes; these the king of Sardinia intended to abridge, and collect into one code, but unfortunately he was not long enough in possession of the island, to accomplish this useful work.—

But where there is an authority above all laws, laws can be but of little ſervice.

The power of the viceroy is very abſolute; he has not only the command of all the military force in the kingdom, but likewiſe preſides with unbounded authority in all civil tribunals; and as he is alſo inveſted with the legantine power, his ſway is equally great in religious matters.

He has the right of nominating to all the great offices in the kingdom; and confirming of all dignities, both civil and eccleſiaſtical.

In viſiting the priſons, a ceremony which he performs with great pomp twice a year, he has the power of liberating whatever priſoners he pleaſes; of reducing or altering their ſentences, their crimes and accuſations having firſt been read over to him.

 Indeed,

Indeed, that there may be ſome appearance of a regard to law and juſtice, his counſellor always attends him on theſe occaſions, to mark out the limits of the law.—This is an officer of very high rank, appointed to aſſiſt the viceroy in his deciſions, where the caſe may appear intricate or dubious; and always is, or ought to be, one of the ableſt lawyers in the iſland. For the moſt part, this office has been given to ſtrangers, who are ſuppoſed to have no kindred or particular connections here, that in giving their judgment they may be free from all prejudice and partiality. He has free admittance into all courts and tribunals, that he may be the better enabled to give the viceroy an account of their proceedings.

The whole military force of Sicily, amounts at preſent, from what I can learn, to 9500 men, about 1200 of which are cavalry. Many of their cities and for-

treſſes

treſſes would require a very numerous garriſon to defend them: particularly Meſſina, Syracuſe, and Palermo: but indeed the ſtate of their fortifications, as well as that of their artillery, is ſuch, that (even if they were inclined) they could make but a ſmall defence.

If this iſland were in the hands of a naval power, I think it is evident, that it muſt command the whole Levant trade:—there are ſeveral little ports at each end of it, beſides the great ones of Trapani, Syracuſe, and Meſſina, which lie pretty near the three angles of the triangle. Whatever ſhips had paſſed either of theſe, the others could be appriſed of in the ſpace of half an hour, by means of ſignal towers, which the Sicilians have erected all around their iſland to warn them againſt ſudden invaſions from the Barbary ſide. Theſe towers are built on every little promontory, within ſight of each other. Fires are always kept ready for lighting, and a person is appointed to watch at each of them, so that the whole island can be alarmed, they assure us, in the space of an hour.

By the bye, we have been witness here of a practice, that appears to be a very iniquitous one, and in the end, I should think, must prove the destruction of our Mediterranean trade. Several ships have put in at this port with English colours, but to our surprise, not one English man on board. These, I find, they call Bandiere men;—perhaps it is a known practice, although, I own, I was an utter stranger to it. They are very numerous in these seas, and carry on a considerable trade through the whole of the Mediterranean, to the great detriment of our own ships. Most of them belong to Genoa and Sicily, though they pass under the name of Minorquins. They purchase

Medi-

Mediterranean passports, I am told, from some of the governors of our garrisons, which entitles them during the term specified in these passports, to trade under English colours. I am assured that the number of these Bandiere men amounts to some hundreds. They have often one or two English sailors on board; or at least some person that speaks the language, to answer when they are challenged. Pray can you tell me if this practice is known in England?

Adieu. The heat has become intolerable, and I am able to write no more;—however, I should not have given it up yet, but my ice is all melted, and I have not the conscience to send out a servant for more: I dare say, you are very glad of it, and wish it had been melted long ago. If this continues, I believe we ourselves shall be melted. The thermometer is above eighty-two, and the heat ſtill ſeems to increaſe.—The ſea has even become too hot for bathing; and it does not at all refreſh us now as it did formerly.

Farewell.

## LETTER XXXIV.

Palermo, July 26th.

WE have now got every thing ready for our departure, and if the wind continues favourable, this is probably the laſt letter I ſhall write you from Sicily. However, I had ſtill a great deal more to ſay, both of the Sicilians and their iſland, and ſhall leave them, I aſſure you, with a good deal of regret.

Two chebecks ſailed this morning for Naples. We had the offer of a paſſage; but had already engaged a little veſſel for ourſelves.—A young nobleman, the marquis of ——, was ſhipped off in one of them, with orders never more to ſet his foot in Palermo. Indeed we are much ſurpriſed that his ſentence is ſo mild, as he

has

has been guilty of a crime which in catholic countries is generally punished with the greatest rigour;—no less than the debauching a nun.—He met with the young lady at a bathing place, about thirty miles from this, where she had been sent from her convent for the recovery of her health; her mother was along with her, but as the two young people were first cousins, and had lived together like brother and sister, the old lady thought there could be no risk in allowing them their wonted familiarity.

The nun soon recovered her health, grew fat, and returned to her convent. This is about six or seven months ago; and it is only a few days since the fatal discovery was made; but alas, it would conceal no longer. He is banished Sicily for life; and his estate, or the greatest part of it, is confiscated. He may think himself happy they have treated him with so much lenity: Had his jury been composed of

priests

prieſts and confeſſors, he muſt have died, without benefit of clergy; for this is the firſt mortal ſin, for which there is neither atonement nor abſolution;—" to lie with a " nun, and yet not be in orders."

The puniſhment of the poor unfortunate girl is not yet determined; however, I am told, it will be a terrible one: probably confinement in a dungeon for ſeven or eight years, without any company but a ſkull and a crucifix; and to live all that time upon bread and water. I ſaw a nun, at Portallegre in Portugal, that had ſuffered this very puniſhment for the ſame crime.

This ſtory has been kept a profound ſecret, and if we had not been on a very intimate footing with ſome people here, we never ſhould have heard of it.

The Sicilians ſtill retain ſome of the Spaniſh cuſtoms, though nothing of their gravity

gravity nor taciturnity; the younger sons of the nobility are stiled Don by their christened names, and the daughters Donna; like our appellation of lord and lady to the sons and daughters of dukes. The eldest son has commonly the title of count or marquis, but they are not all counts as in France and Germany, where I have seen six counts in one house, and very near twice the number of barons in another.

One of the most common titles here, as well as at Naples, is that of Prince; and although these were only created by Philip II. of Spain, they take rank of all the other nobility, some of whom, particularly the counts, carry their origin as far back as the time of the Normans, and look with great contempt on these upstart Princes. The dukes and marquisses are not so old: the first were created by Charles V, and the second, though an inferior title, by King Alphonso, in the fifteenth century.—

So that the dignity of the Sicilian titles may be said to be in the inverse ratio of their antiquities.

The luxury of the people here, like that of the Neapolitans, consists chiefly in their equipages and horses; but by a wise law of the King of Sardinia, which I am surprised should still remain in force, the viceroy alone is allowed to drive in the city with six horses; the prætor, the archbishop, and president of the parliament with four; all the rest of the nobility are restricted to two. But this is only within the gates of Palermo; and when they go to the country, there is none of them that drive with less than four: besides, every family of distinction has at least two or three carriages in daily use; for no man of fashion is so unpolite as to refuse his wife a chariot of her own, of which she has the entire command; (without this the Marino could never subsist) and the upper servants of the first

families

families would be just as much ashamed to be seen on foot as their masters.—We took the liberty to ridicule the folly of this practice: they allow of its absurdity, and wish to break through it; but who is to lead the way? We even prevailed with some of the young nobility, which I assure you was no small condescension, to walk the streets with us during the illuminations; but even this condescension shewed the folly of the prejudice in a stronger light than if they had refused us; for they would not be prevailed on to stir out, till they had sent their servants about ten yards before them, with large wax flambeaux, although the whole city was in a flame of light. You may believe we did not spare them upon this occasion; but it was all to no purpose. However, it is possible that we may overlook many customs of our own, that are not less ridiculous; for ridicule for the most part is relative, and depends only on time and place.—Perhaps you may remember the

Prince

Prince of Anamaboo;—I should like to hear the account he would give of the English nation in his own country; for some of our customs struck him in a still more ridiculous light.—Walking out in St. James's Park, in the afternoon, he observed one of his acquaintance driving in a phaeton with four horses. The Prince burst into a violent fit of laughing:—when they asked him what was the matter?—"Vat "the devil, (said the Prince in his bad "English) has that fellow eat so much "dinner that now it takes four horses to "carry him?—I rode out with him this "morning, and he was then so light, that "van little horse ran away with him.—He "must either be a great fool or a great "glutton."—Another time they insisted on the Prince going to the play.—He went; but he soon tired of it, and returned to his companions.—"Well, Prince, (said they) "what did you see?"—"Vat did I see, "(replied

"(replied he with the utmost contempt) I "did see some men playing de fiddle—and "some men playing de fool."

I only infer from this, that it is with some degree of caution we should ridicule the customs of other nations: a Sicilian, perhaps, would laugh with as much justice at many of our customs;—that, for instance, of obliging people to drink when they have no inclination to it;—that in the North, of eating Soland geese before dinner, to give them an appetite;—that of physicians and lawyers wearing enormous wigs, and many others that will naturally occur to you, none of which appear in the least ridiculous to the people that practise them; who would no doubt defend them as strenuously as the Sicilians do the necessity of carrying flambeaux before them during the great illumination.—Indeed, they have just now given us an admirable ſpecimen of ſome of our ridicules, in one of their opera-dances, with which we have been a good deal entertained.

I believe I told you that the dancers are lately come from England: they have brought upon the ſtage many of the capital London characters:—The bucks, the maccaronies, the prigs, the cits, and ſome others ſtill more reſpectable: theſe are well ſupported, and afford a good deal of laughing. But I am interrupted, otherwiſe I ſhould have given you a more particular account of them. Adieu. The heat is intolerable; and there is no poſſibility of walking out.—We complain without reaſon of our own climate; and King Charles's obſervation I am perſuaded was juſt; "That there is hardly any climate, where, throughout the year, we can have ſo much exerciſe in the open air."

Ever your's.

## LETTER XXXV.

Palermo, July 27th.

THE Sicilians are animated in conversation, and their action for the most part is so just and so expressive of their sentiments, that without hearing what is said, one may comprehend the subject of their discourse. We used to think the French and Neapolitans great adepts in this art; but they are much outdone by the Sicilians, both in the variety and justness of their gesticulation.

The origin of this custom they carry so far back as the time of the earliest tyrants of Syracuse, who, to prevent conspiracies, had forbid their subjects, under the most severe penalties, to be seen in parties talking together. This obliged them to invent a me-a method of communicating their ſentiments by dumb ſhew, which they pretend has been tranſmitted from generation to generation ever ſince.

I think it is not at all improbable that this cuſtom too may have given the firſt idea of comedy; as we find, that ſome ſhort time after, Epicarmus, a native of that city, was the author of this invention.

The Sicilians till lately retained a great many fooliſh and ſuperſtitious cuſtoms; but particularly in their marriage and funeral ceremonies: it would be tedious to give you an account of all theſe; ſome of them are ſtill practiſed in the wild and mountainous parts of the iſland.—As ſoon as the marriage ceremony is performed, two of the attendants are ready to cram a ſpoonful of honey into the mouths of the bride and bridegroom; pronouncing it emblematical of their love and union, which they hope will ever continue as ſweet to their ſouls, as that honey is to their palates.— They then begin to throw handfuls of wheat upon them, which is continued all the way, to the houſe of the bridegroom. This is probably the remains of ſome ancient rite to Ceres, their favourite divinity, and they think it cannot fail of procuring them a numerous progeny :—however, the Sicilian women have no occaſion for any charm to promote this, as, in general, they are abundantly prolific even without it. Fazzello gives an account of women having frequently upwards of forty children; and Carrera mentions one who had forty-ſeven.

The young couple are not allowed to taſte of the marriage-feaſt; this they pretend is to teach them patience and temperance; but when dinner is finiſhed, a great bone is preſented to the bridegroom by the bride's father, or one of her neareſt relations, who pronounces theſe words: "*Rodi tu queſt'*

"*oſſo,*

"*osso*, &c. Pick you this bone, for you have "now taken in hand to pick one, which you "will find much harder and of more dif- "ficult digestion."—Perhaps this may have given rise to the common saying, when one has undertaken any thing arduous or difficult, that "He has got a bone to "pick."

The Sicilians, like most other nations in Europe, carefully avoid marrying in the month of May, and look upon such marriages as extremely inauspicious. This piece of superstition is as old, perhaps older than the time of the Romans, by whose authors it is frequently mentioned; and by whom it has been transmitted to almost every nation in Europe. It is somewhat unaccountable, that so ridiculous an idea, which can have no foundation in nature, should have stood its ground for so many ages.—There are indeed other customs still more trivial, that are not less universal.—

That of making April fools on the first day of that month; the ceremony of the cake on Twelfth-night; and some others that will occur to you, of which, no more than this, I have ever been able to learn the origin.

The marriages of the Sicilian nobility are celebrated with great magnificence; and the number of elegant carriages produced on these occasions is astonishing. I wanted to discover when this great luxury in carriages had taken its rise; and have found an account of the marriage of the daughter of one of their viceroys to the duke of Bivona, in the year 1551. It is described by one Elenco, who was a spectator of the ceremony. He says the ladies as well as gentlemen were all mounted on fine horses, sumptuously caparisoned, and preceded by pages: that there were only three carriages in the city, which were used by invalids who were not able to ride on horseback. These

he

he calls *Carette*, which word now ſignifies a little cart.

The Sicilian ladies marry very young, and frequently live to ſee the fifth or ſixth generation. You will expect, no doubt, that I ſhould ſay ſomething of their beauty:—In general, they are ſprightly and agreeable; and in moſt parts of Italy they would be eſteemed handſome.—A Neapolitan or a Roman would ſurely pronounce them ſo.—But a Piedmonteſe would declare them very ordinary;—ſo indeed would moſt Engliſhmen.—Nothing ſo vague as our ideas of female beauty: they change in every climate; and the criterion is no where to be found.—

"Aſk where's the North?—at York, 'tis on
the Tweed,
"In Scotland at the Orcades, and there,
"At Nova Zembla, or the Lord knows where."

No two nations,—perhaps no two men, have affixed precisely the same characteristics; and every one exalts his idea of it, according to the beauty of the women he is accustomed to see; so that even the same person may sometimes appear beautiful, sometimes ugly, just in proportion as we have seen others that are more or less so.— I remember, after making the tour of Savoy and the Lower Valais, every woman we met in Switzerland appeared an angel. The same thing happens in travelling through some parts of Germany; and you will easily recollect the surprising difference betwixt a beauty at Milan and one at Turin, although these places lie adjacent to each other.—It is a pity that the Juno of Zeuxis has been lost, if it were no more than to have shewn us the notion the antients had of a perfect beauty. Indeed, the Venus of Medicis has been considered as a model of perfection,—but it is surely absurd;—for who

who ever heard of a perfect beauty of five feet high!—the very idea is ridiculous; and whatever figure her goddefship might make amongft the ancient divinities, in the pantheon at Rome, I am afraid fhe would cut but a forry one amongft the modern ones, in that of London.—In fhort, I believe we may fafely conclude, that beauty is a relative quality, and the *To kalon* is no longer the fame, no more in a phyfical than a moral fenfe, in any two places on the globe.

The ladies here have remarkable fine hair, and they underftand how to drefs and adorn it to the greateft advantage. It is now only ufed as an embellifhment; but in former times we are told, that, like that of Sampfon, it was found to be the ftrength and protection of their country.—There is a paradox for you, that all the wife men of the Eaft could hardly folve.—Their hiftorians relate, (in whofe reign I believe is

rather

rather dubious) that this city had suffered a long siege from the Saracens, and was greatly reduced by famine; but, what distressed them still more, there were no materials to be found for making bowstrings, and they were on the point of surrendering.—In this dilemma, a patriotic dame stepped forth, and proposed to the women, that the whole of them should cut off their hair, and twist it into bowstrings: This was immediately complied with.—The heroism of the women, you know, must ever excite that of the men.—The besieged, animated by this gallant sacrifice of the fair, renewed their defence with such vigour, that the assailants were beat off; and a reinforcement soon after arriving, the city was saved.—The ladies still value themselves on this story, which you may believe has not been forgotten by their bards.— "The hair of our ladies (says one of their "quaint poets) is still employed in the "same office; but now it discharges no

" other ſhafts but thoſe of Cupid; and the " only cords it forms are the cords of " love."

The Sicilians are much fonder of ſtudy than their neighbours on the continent; and their education is much more attended to. We were a good deal ſurpriſed to find, that inſtead of that frivolity and nothingneſs, which ſo often conſtitute the converſation of the Italian nobility, here their delight was to talk on ſubjects of literature, of hiſtory, of politics, but chiefly of poetry; for the other branches of knowlege and ſcience are only general: this is the only one that may be ſaid to be univerſal. Every perſon, in ſome period of his life, is ſure to be inſpired; and a lover is never believed ſo long as he can ſpeak of his paſſion in proſe; and, contrary to our way of reaſoning, is only reckoned true in proportion as he is poetical. Thus, inſpiration,

ration, you ſee, has here become the teſt of truth.

We were aſtoniſhed on our firſt arrival at Palermo, to hear ourſelves addreſſed in Engliſh by ſome of the young nobility; but ſtill more ſo, to find them intimately acquainted with many of our celebrated poets and philoſophers.—Milton, Shakeſpeare, Dryden, Pope, Bacon, Bolingbroke we found in ſeveral libraries, not in the tranſlation, but generally in the beſt editions of the original.

Our language, indeed, has become ſo much in vogue, that it is now looked upon as no immaterial part of a polite education: the viceroy, the Marquis Fogliano, a man of great merit and humanity, has made ſome of our authors his favourite ſtudy, and greatly encourages the progreſs it is making in his kingdom. Many of of the nobility ſpeak it a little; and ſome of them even with eaſe and fluency, although they have never been out of their iſland. The Marquis Natali, the Counts Statela and Buſchemi, the Duke of St. Micheli, &c.; in whoſe company we have enjoyed a great deal of pleaſure, and whoſe knowlege and erudition is the leaſt part of their praiſe. Adieu.

Your's, &c.

## LETTER XXXVI.

Palermo, July 28th.

I HAD almost forgot to say any thing of the opera:—It would have been very ungrateful, for we have been much delighted with it.—The first and second man, are both admirable singers, and I make no doubt you will have them in London in a few years; neither of them are as yet known, and I dare say at present they might be engaged for a very moderate price; but in Italy they will soon be taught to estimate their value.—The name of the first is Pacherotti; he is very young, and an entire stranger in the musical world; yet I am persuaded, that after he has been heard on the different theatres in Italy, he will be esteemed one of their capital performers. His excellence is the pathetic, at present too

too much neglected on most theatres; and indeed, I think, he gives more expression to his *cantabile* airs, and makes his hearers feel more, because he feels more himself, than any that I have seen in Italy. He indeed addresses himself to the heart, while most of the modern performers sing only to the fancy.

The first woman is Gabrieli; who is certainly the greatest singer in the world; and those that sing on the same theatre with her, must be capital, otherwise they never can be attended to. This indeed has been the fate of all the other performers, except Pacherotti; and he too gave himself up for lost, on hearing her first performance.—It happened to be an air of execution, exactly adapted to her voice, which she exerted in so astonishing a manner, that before it was half done, poor Pacherotti burst out a crying, and ran in behind the scenes; lamenting that he

had

had dared to appear on the ſame ſtage with ſo wonderful a ſinger; where his ſmall talents muſt not only be loſt, but where he muſt ever be accuſed of a preſumption, which he hoped was foreign to his character.

It was with ſome difficulty they could prevail on him to appear again, but from an applauſe well merited, both from his talents and his modeſty, he ſoon began to pluck up a little courage; and in the ſinging of a tender air, addreſſed to Gabrieli in the character of a lover, even ſhe herſelf, as well as the audience, is ſaid to have been moved.

Indeed, in theſe very pathetic pieces, I am ſurpriſed that the power of the muſic does not ſometimes altogether overcome the deluſion of character; for when you are maſter of the language, and allow the united power of the poetry, the action, and

the

the music, to have its full force on the mind, the effect is wonderfully great.—However I have never heard that this happened completely but once; and it was no less a singer than Farinelli that produced it.—He appeared in the character of a young captive hero, and in a tender air was soliciting mercy for his mistress and himself, of a stern and cruel tyrant who had made them his prisoners. The person that acted the tyrant was so perfectly overcome by the melting strains of Farinelli, that instead of refusing his request as he ought to have done, he entirely forgot his character, burst into tears, and caught him in his arms.

The performance of Gabrieli is so generally known and admired, that it is needless to say any thing to you on that subject. Her wonderful execution and volubility of voice have long been the admiration of Italy, and has even obliged them to invent a new term to express it; and would ſhe exert herſelf as much to pleaſe as to aſtoniſh, ſhe might almoſt perform the wonders that have been aſcribed to Orpheus and Timotheus; but it happens, luckily perhaps for the repoſe of mankind, that her caprice is, if poſſible, even greater than her talents, and has made her ſtill more contemptible than theſe have made her celebrated. By this means, her character has often proved a ſufficient antidote, both to the charms of her voice and thoſe of her perſon, which are indeed almoſt equally powerful; but if theſe had been united to the qualities of a modeſt and an amiable mind, ſhe muſt have made dreadful havoc in the world. However, with all her faults, ſhe is certainly the moſt dangerous ſyren of modern times, and has made more conqueſts, I ſuppoſe, than any one woman breathing.

It is but juſtice to add, that contrary to the generality of her profeſſion, ſhe is by no

means

means selfish or mercenary; but on the contrary, has given many singular proofs of generosity and disinterestedness. She is very rich; from the bounty, as is supposed, of the last emperor, who was fond of having her at Vienna; but she was at last banished that city, as she has likewise been most of those in Italy, from the broils and squabbles that her intriguing spirit, perhaps still more than her beauty, had excited. There are a great many anecdotes concerning her, that would not make an unentertaining volume; and, I am told, either are, or will soon be published.

. . . . .

Although she is considerably upwards of thirty, on the stage she scarcely appears to be eighteen; and this art of appearing young, is none of the most contemptible that she possesses.—When she is in good humour, and really chuses to exert herself, there is nothing in music that I have ever heard, to be compared to her performance; for ſhe ſings to the heart as well as the fancy, when ſhe pleaſes; and ſhe then commands every paſſion with unbounded ſway. But ſhe is ſeldom capable of exerciſing theſe wonderful powers; and her caprice and her talents exerting themſelves by turns, have given her, all her life, the ſingular fate of becoming alternately an object of admiration and of contempt.

Her powers in acting and reciting, are ſcarcely inferior to thoſe of her ſinging; ſometimes, a few words in the recitative, with a ſimple accompaniment only, produces an effect, that I have never been ſenſible of from any other performer; and inclines me to believe what Rouſſeau advances on this branch of muſic, which with us is ſo much deſpiſed. She owes much of her merit to the inſtructions ſhe received from Meteſtaſio, particularly in acting and reciting; and he allows that ſhe does more juſtice to his operas than any other actreſs that ever attempted them.

Her caprice is ſo fixed and ſo ſtubborn, that neither intereſt, nor flattery, nor threats, nor puniſhments, have the leaſt power over it; and it appears, that treating her with reſpect or contempt, have an equal tendency to increaſe it.

It is ſeldom that ſhe condeſcends to exert theſe wonderful talents; but moſt particularly if ſhe imagines that ſuch an exertion is expected. And inſtead of ſinging her airs as other actreſſes do, for the moſt part ſhe only hums them over, *a mezza voce*. And no art whatever is capable of making her ſing when ſhe does not chuſe it.

The moſt ſucceſsful expedient has ever been found, to prevail on her favourite lover, for ſhe always has one, to place him-

 ſelf

ſelf in the center of the pit, or the front box; and if they are on good terms, which is ſeldom the caſe, ſhe will addreſs her tender airs to him, and exert herſelf to the utmoſt.—Her preſent enamorato promiſed to give us this ſpecimen of his power over her; he took his place accordingly; but Gabrieli, probably ſuſpecting the connivance, would take no notice of him; ſo that even this expedient does not always ſucceed.

The viceroy, who is fond of muſic, has tried every method with her to no purpoſe. Sometime ago he gave a great dinner to the principal nobility of Palermo, and ſent an invitation to Gabrieli to be of the party. Every other perſon arrived at the hour of invitation. The viceroy ordered dinner to be kept back, and ſent to let her know that the company waited her. The meſſenger found her reading in bed;—ſhe ſaid ſhe was ſorry for having made the company

wait,

wait, and begged he would make her apology, but that really ſhe had entirely forgot her engagement.

The viceroy would have forgiven this piece of inſolence, but, when the company came to the opera, Gabrieli repeated her part with the moſt perfect negligence and indifference, and ſung all her airs in what they call *ſotto voce*, that is, ſo low, that they can ſcarcely be heard. The viceroy was offended; but as he is a good-tempered man, he was loth to make uſe of authority; but at laſt, by a perſeverance in this inſolent ſtubbornneſs, ſhe obliged him to threaten her with puniſhment in caſe ſhe any longer refuſed to ſing.

On this ſhe grew more obſtinate than ever, declaring that force and authority ſhould never ſucceed with her; that he might make her cry, but that he never could make her ſing. The viceroy then ſent her to priſon, where ſhe remained twelve days. During which time, ſhe gave magnificent entertainments every day; paid the debts of all the poor priſoners, and diſtributed large ſums in charity. The viceroy was obliged to give up ſtruggling with her, and ſhe was at laſt ſet at liberty amidſt the acclamations of the poor.—Luckily for us, ſhe is at preſent in good humour, and ſometimes exerts herſelf to the utmoſt of her power.

She ſays ſhe has ſeveral times been on terms with the managers of our opera, but thinks ſhe ſhall never be able to pluck up reſolution enough to go to England. What do you think is her reaſon?—It is by no means a bad one. She ſays ſhe cannot command her caprice; but, for the moſt part, that it commands her; and that there, ſhe could have no opportunity of indulging it:—For, ſays ſhe, were I to take it into my head not to ſing, I am told the people

people there would certainly mob me, and perhaps break my bones;—now I like to ſleep in a ſound ſkin, although it ſhould even be in a priſon.—She alleges too that it is not always caprice that prevents her from ſinging; but that it often depends upon phyſical cauſes; and this indeed I can readily believe: for that wonderful flexibility of voice that runs with ſuch rapidity and neatneſs through the moſt minute diviſions, and produces almoſt inſtantaneouſly ſo great a variety of modulation, muſt ſurely depend on the very niceſt tone of the fibres. And if theſe are in the ſmalleſt degree relaxed, or their elaſticity diminiſhed; how is it poſſible that their contractions and expanſions can ſo readily obey the will, as to produce theſe effects?—The opening of the glottis which forms the voice is extremely ſmall, and in every variety of tone, its diameter muſt ſuffer a ſenſible change; for the ſame diameter muſt ever produce the ſame tone:—So wonderfully

minute

minute are its contractions and dilatations, that Dr. Keil, I think, computes, that in ſome voices, its opening, not more than the tenth of an inch, is divided into upwards of 1200 parts, the different ſound of every one of which is perceptible to an exact ear. Now, what a nice tenſion of fibres muſt this require!—I ſhould imagine every the moſt minute change in the air, muſt cauſe a ſenſible difference, and that in our foggy climate the fibres would be in danger of loſing this wonderful ſenſibility; or at leaſt, that they would very often be put out of tune. It is not the ſame caſe with an ordinary voice; where the variety of diviſions run through, and the volubility with which they are executed, bear no proportion to thoſe of a Gabrieli.

One of the ballets of our opera, is a repreſentation of Vauxhall gardens, and this is the third time I have ſeen Vauxhall brought upon the Italian theatre; at Turin, at at Naples, and here. The gardens are well reprefented, and the idea muft have been given by fome perfon that had been on the fpot. A variety of good Englifh figures are brought in: fome with large frizzled wigs fticking half a yard out behind their necks; fome with little cut fcratches, that look extremely ridiculous. Some come in cracking their whips, with buckfkin breeches and jockey caps. Some are armed with great oaken fticks; their hair tied up in enormous clubs, and ftocks that fwell their necks to double its natural fize. But what affords the principal part of the entertainment is, three quakers who are duped by three ladies of the town, in concert with three jack tars, their lovers.—Thefe characters, as you may believe, are much exaggerated, though, upon the whole, they are fupported with humour, and have afforded us a good deal of laughing; however, we were hurt to fee the refpectable

character

character of quakers turned into ſuch ridicule; and as the people here were altogether unacquainted with it, we have been at ſome pains to explain to them the ſimplicity and purity of their manners, and the incorruptible integrity of their principles.

Although the Sicilians in general are a good ſort of people, and ſeem to be endowed with a large ſhare of philanthropy and urbanity; yet it muſt be owned they have no great affection for their neighbours on the continent; and indeed the diſlike is altogether reciprocal.—It is ſomewhat ſingular; I am afraid not much for the honour of human nature; that through all Europe, the two neighbouring nations have a perpetual jarring with each other.—I could heartily wiſh that we had been an exception from this rule; but am ſorry to ſee, from our news-papers, which are ſent to

the

the nobility of this city, that at preſent we are rather the moſt diſtinguiſhed for it; at leaſt our animoſities, if there really are any, make by much the greateſt noiſe of all.—We have often been aſked by foreigners what was the ground of the mighty quarrel, that ſuch torrents of the moſt illiberal abuſe have been poured out by a people ſo celebrated for liberality of ſentiment; and it is with difficulty we can perſuade them, that although from the papers, this ſometimes appears to be the voice of the nation, yet in fact, it is only confined to a ſet of the moſt worthleſs and deſpicable incendiaries; like him who ſet the houſe in a flame, on purpoſe to pilfer during the conflagration.—But the abuſe that is levelled at the king, ſurpriſes them more than all the reſt; and you cannot conceive their amazement and indignation when we aſſured them, that notwithſtanding all this, he was the moſt vir-

tuous

tuous and benevolent prince on earth.—Then, exclaimed a Sicilian nobleman, you must certainly be the most damnable people on the globe.—I was a good deal struck with the suddenness of the charge; and it was not without many explanations of the liberty of our constitution, and particularly that of the press, that I could prevail with him to retract his sentiments; and think more favourably of us.—Still he insisted, that so egregious an abuse of this liberty, was only a farther proof of his position; and that there must be something essentially wrong, in a nation that could allow of such abuse levelled at the most sacred of all characters: the highest virtue united to the highest station. We assured him, that what he heard, was only the voice of the most abandoned and profligate wretches in the nation; who, taking advantage of the great freedom of the press, had often made these news-papers the vehicles of the most deteſtable ſedition. That both the king and queen were beloved by all their ſubjects, at leaſt by all thoſe of worth;—that they never were ſpoken of, but as the moſt perfect model of conjugal union and happineſs, as well as of every ſocial endowment; and that they could have no enemies, but the enemies of virtue.

However, after all, we could but patch up a peace with him. He could not comprehend (he ſaid) how the voice of a few incendiaries ſhould be louder than the general voice of the nation.—We told him, that people who were pleaſed commonly held their tongue; and that ſedition and libel ever made a greater noiſe than panegyric; juſt as the fire-bell is rung louder, and is more liſtened to than the bell for rejoicing.

Adieu.

Adieu. Our pilot ſays the wind is not fair, ſo that poſſibly we may ſtill ſtay a day or two longer.

Ever your's.

# LETTER XXXVII.

Palermo, July 29th.

WERE I to enter upon the natural hiſtory of this iſland, it would lead me into a vaſt field of ſpeculation, for which I have neither time nor abilities: However, a variety of objects ſtruck us as we travelled along, that it may not be amiſs to give you ſome little account of.—There are a variety of mineral waters, almoſt through the whole of Sicily. Many of theſe are boiling hot; others ſtill more ſingular, are of a degree of cold ſuperior to that of ice, and yet never freeze.

In ſeveral places, they have fountains that throw up a kind of oil on their ſurface, which is of great uſe to the peaſants, who burn it in their lamps, and uſe it to many other purpoſes; but there is ſtill a more remarkable one near Nicoſia which is called *il fonte Canalotto.* It is covered with a thick ſcum of a kind of pitch, which amongſt the country people is eſteemed a ſovereign remedy in rheumatic, and many other complaints.

The water of a ſmall lake near Naſo is celebrated for dying black every thing that is put into it; and this it is ſaid to perform without the mixture of any other ingredient, although the water itſelf is remarkably pure and tranſparent.

They have a variety of ſulphureous baths, like thoſe near Naples, where the patient is thrown into a profuſe ſweat, only from the heat of the vapour. The moſt celebrated are thoſe of Sciaccia, and on the mountain of St. Cologero; not in the neighbourhood of Ætna, as I expected,

but

but at a great diſtance from that mountain. But indeed I am much inclined to believe, that not only mount Ætna, but the greateſt part of Sicily, and almoſt the whole of the circumjacent iſlands, have been originally formed by ſubterraneous fire; but I ſhall have an opportunity of ſpeaking more largely on this ſubject, when I give you an account of the country round Naples.

I have obſerved lava, pumice, and tufa in many parts of Sicily, at a great diſtance from Ætna; and there are a variety both of mountains and valleys that ſtill emit a hot vapour, and produce ſprings of boiling water.

About a mile and a half to the weſt of this city, at a ſmall beach where we often go a ſwimming, there are many ſprings of warm water, that riſe even within the ſea, at the depth of five or ſix feet. We were at firſt a good deal ſurpriſed to find ourſelves almoſt inſtantaneouſly both in the hot and cold bath; for at one ſtroke we commonly paſſed through the hot water, which only extends for a few feet around the ſpring. It gave us a momentary glow, and produced a very odd, uncouth ſenſation, by no means an agreeable one. I mentioned this ſingularity to ſeveral gentlemen here, who tell me they have obſerved the ſame thing.

Not a great way from this is a celebrated fountain, called *Il Mar Dolce*, where there are ſome remains of an ancient naumachia; and in the mountain above it, they ſhew you a cavern, where a gigantic ſkeleton is ſaid to have been found: however, it fell to duſt when they attempted to remove it;—Fazzello ſays, its teeth were the only part that reſiſted the impreſſion of the air; that he procured two of them, and that they weighed near two ounces.—There are many ſuch ſtories

to

to be met with in the Sicilian legends, as it ſeems to be an univerſal belief, that this iſland was once inhabited by giants; but although we have made diligent enquiry, we have never yet been able to procure a ſight of any of theſe gigantic bones which are ſaid to be ſtill preſerved in many parts of the iſland. Had there been any foundation for this, I think it is probable, they muſt have found their way into ſome of the muſeums; but this is not the caſe; nor indeed have we met with any perſon of ſenſe and credibility that could ſay they had ſeen any of them. We had been aſſured at Naples, that an entire ſkeleton, upwards of ten feet high, was preſerved in the muſeum of Palermo; but there is no ſuch thing there, nor I believe any where elſe in the iſland.—This muſeum is well furniſhed both with antiques and articles of natural hiſtory, but is not ſuperior to what we have ſeen in many other places.

The number of ſouls in Palermo are computed at about 150,000. Thoſe of the whole iſland, by the laſt numeration, amounted to 1,123,163; of which number there are about 50,000 that belong to the different monaſteries and religious orders. The number of houſes are computed at 268,120, which makes betwixt five and ſix to a houſe.

The great ſtanding commodity of Sicily, which has ever conſtituted the riches of the iſland, was their crops of wheat; but they cultivate many other branches of commerce, though none that could bear any proportion to this, were it under a free government, and exportation allowed. Their method of preſerving their grain will appear ſomewhat ſingular to our farmers: inſtead of expoſing it, as we do, to the open air, they are at the greateſt pains to exclude it entirely from it.—In many places, where the ſoil is dry, particularly near Agrigentum, they have dug large pits or caverns in the rock. Theſe open by a ſmall hole at top, and ſwell to a great width below; here they pour down their grain, after it has been made exceedingly dry; and ramming it hard, they cover up the hole, to protect it from rain; and they aſſure us it will preſerve in this manner for many years.

The Soda is a plant that is much cultivated, and turns out to conſiderable account. This is the vegetable, that by the action of fire, is afterwards converted into mirrors and chryſtals. Great quantities of it are ſent every year to ſupply the glaſs-houſes at Venice.—They have likewiſe a conſiderable trade in liquorice, rice, figs, raiſins, and currants, the beſt of which grow amongſt the extinguiſhed volcanoes of the Lipari Iſlands. Their honey is, I think, the higheſt flavoured I have ever ſeen; in ſome parts of the iſland even ſuperior to that of Minorca: this is owing, no doubt, to the quantity of aromatic plants, with which this beautiful country is every where overſpread. This honey is gathered three months in the year; July, Auguſt, and October. It is found by the peaſants in the hollows of trees and rocks; and is eſteemed of a ſuperior quality to that produced under the tyranny of man.—The country of the Leſſer Hybla is ſtill, as formerly, the part of the iſland that is moſt celebrated for honey. The Count Statela made us a preſent of ſome of it, gathered on his brother the Prince of Spaccaforno's eſtate, which lies near the ruins of that city.

Sugar is now no article of the Sicilian commerce, though a ſmall quantity of it is ſtill manufactured for home conſumption; but the plantations of the ſugar-cane, I am told, thrive well in ſeveral parts of the iſland.

The

The juice of liquorice is prepared both here and in Calabria, and is ſent to the northern countries of Europe, where it is uſed for colds.—The juice is ſqueezed out of the roots; after which it is boiled to a conſiſtency, and formed into cakes, which are packed up with bay-leaves in the ſame order that we receive them.

In ſome of the northern parts of the iſland, I am told, they find the ſhell-fiſh that produces a kind of flax, of which gloves and ſtockings are made; but theſe too are found in greater quantities in Calabria.

Their plantations of oranges, lemons, bergamots, almonds, &c. produce no inconſiderable branch of commerce. The piſtachio-nut too is much cultivated in many parts of the iſland, and with great ſucceſs. Theſe trees, like many others, are male and female: the male is called *Scornobecco*, and is always barren; but unless a quantity of these are mixed in every plantation, the pistachio-tree never bears a nut.—But of all the variety that is cultivated in Sicily, the manna-tree is esteemed the most profitable; it resembles the ash, and is I believe of that species. About the beginning of August, during the season of the greatest heat, they make an incision in the bark, near to the root of the tree; a thick whitish liquor is immediately discharged from the wound, which soon hardens in the sun; when it is carefully taken off and gathered into boxes. They renew these incisions every day during the season, observing, however, only to wound one side of the tree; the other side they reserve for the summer following.

The cantharides-fly is a Sicilian commodity: it is found on several trees of Ætna, whose

whoſe juice is ſuppoſed to have a corroſive or abſterſive quality, particularly the pine and the fig-tree; and I am told the cantharides of Mount Ætna are reckoned preferable to thoſe of Spain.

The marbles of Sicily would afford a great ſource of opulence, were there any encouragement to work the quarries: of theſe they have an infinite variety, and of the fineſt ſorts. I have ſeen ſome of them little inferior to the giall and verd antique, that is now ſo precious. The beautiful yellow columns you muſt have obſerved in the royal chapel of Caſſerto are of the firſt kind. They have likewiſe ſome that very much reſemble lapis lazuli and porphyry.

At Centorbi they find a kind of ſoft ſtone that diſſolves in water, and is uſed in waſhing inſtead of ſoap, from which property it is called *Pietra Saponaro.* They likewiſe find here, as well as in Calabria, the celebrated ſtone, which, upon being watered and expoſed to a pretty violent degree of heat, produces a plentiful crop of muſhrooms:—But it would be endleſs to give you an account of all the various commodities and curious productions of this iſland; Ætna alone affords a greater number than many of the moſt extenſive kingdoms, and is no leſs an epitome of the whole earth in its ſoil and climate, than in the variety of its productions.—Beſides the corn, the wine, the oil, the ſilk, the ſpice, and delicious fruits of its lower region; the beautiful foreſts, the flocks, the game, the tar, the cork, the honey, of its ſecond; the ſnow and ice of its third; it affords from its caverns a variety of mineral and other productions; cinnabar, mercury, ſulphur, allum, nitre, and vitriol; ſo that this wonderful mountain at the ſame time

produces

produces every neceſſary, and every luxury of life.

Its firſt region covers their tables with all the delicacies that the earth produces; its ſecond ſupplies them with game, cheeſe, butter, honey; and not only furniſhes wood of every kind for building their ſhips and houſes, but likewiſe an inexhauſtible ſtore of excellent fewel; and as the third region, with its ice and ſnow, keeps them freſh and cool during the heat of ſummer, ſo this contributes equally to keep them warm and comfortable during the cold of winter.

Thus, you ſee, the variety of climates is not confined to Ætna itſelf; but, in obedience to the voice of man, deſcends from that mountain; and, mingling the violence of their extremes, diffuſes the moſt benign influences all over the iſland, tempering each

each other to moderation, and ſoftening the rigours of every ſeaſon.

We are not then to be ſurpriſed at the obſtinate attachment of the people to this mountain, and that all his terrors have not been able to drive them away from him: for although he ſometimes chaſtiſes; yet, like an indulgent parent, he mixes ſuch bleſſings along with his chaſtiſements, that their affections can never be eſtranged; for at the ſame time that he threatens with a rod of iron, he pours down upon them all the bleſſings of the age of gold.

Adieu.—We are now going to pay our reſpects to the viceroy, and make our farewell viſits.—This ceremony never fails to throw a damp on my ſpirits; but I have ſeldom found it ſo ſtrong as at preſent, there being little or no probability that we ſhall ever ſee again a number of worthy

people

people we are juſt now going to take leave of; or that we ſhall ever have it in our power to make any return for the many civilities we have received from them.

Farewell. The wind we are told is fair, and I ſhall probably be the bearer of this to the continent, from whence you may ſoon expect to hear from, &c.

## LETTER XXXVIII.

Naples, August 1ſt.

AFTER two days delightful ſailing, we have again arrived in this city; where, to our infinite joy, we have found all the worthy friends we had left behind us. This indeed was neceſſary, to wipe out the impreſſions which the leaving of Sicily had occaſioned. We ſhall ſtill remain here, at leaſt for three months, till the ſeaſon of the *Mal Aria* is entirely over. You know the danger of travelling through the Campania during that ſeaſon; which although it is looked upon by many of our learned doctors as a vulgar error, yet we certainly ſhall not ſubmit ourſelves to the experiment.

We

We propose to pass the winter at Rome, where we shall probably find occupation enough for four or five months.—From thence by Loretto, Bologna, &c. to Venice; the old beaten track.—We shall then leave the parched fields of Italy, for the delightful cool mountains of Switzerland;—where liberty and simplicity, long since banished from polished nations, still flourish in their original purity; where the temperature and moderation of the climate, and that of the inhabitants, are mutually emblematical of each other.—For whilst other nations are scorched by the heat of the sun, and the still more scorching heats of tyranny and superstition; here the genial breezes for ever fan the air, and heighten that alacrity and joy which liberty and innocence alone can inspire;—here the genial flow of the soul has never yet been check'd by the idle and useless refinements of art; but opens and expands itself to all the calls of affection and benevolence.—But I must stop. You know my old attachment to that primitive country.— It never fails to run away with me. We propose then, to make this the scene of our summer pleasures; and by that time, I can foresee, we shall be heartily tired of Art, and shall begin again to languish after Nature. It is she alone that can give any real or lasting pleasure, and in all our pursuits of happiness, if she is not our guide, we never can attain our end.

Adieu my dear friend. You have been our faithful companion during this Tour; and have not contributed a little to its pleasure. If it has afforded equal entertainment to you, we shall beg of you still to accompany us through the rest of our travels. A man must have a miserable imagination indeed, that can be in solitude, whilst he has such friends to converse with; the consideration of it soon removes the mountains and seas that separate us,

and

and produces these sympathetic feelings, which are the only equivalent for the real absence of a friend; for I never sit down to write, but I see you placed on the opposite side of the table, and suppose that we are just talking over the transactions of the day. And without your presence to animate me, how is it possible that I could have had patience to write these enormous epistles?—Adieu. We are soon going to make some excursions through the kingdom of Naples; and if they produce any thing worthy of your observation, we must beg that you will still submit to be one of the party.

I ever am,

Most sincerely and affectionately, your's,

PAT. BRYDONE.

FINIS.

9

Lightning Source UK Ltd.
Milton Keynes UK
UKHW012227110219
337137UK00006B/1229/P

9 780365 372615